WELSH RUGBY CAPTAINS

WELSH RUGBY CAPTAINS

With
Alun Wyn Bevan and Huw Evans

Gomer

Published in 2010 by
Gomer Press, Llandysul, Ceredigion, SA44 4JL

ISBN 978 1 84851 211 5

A CIP record for this title is available from the British Library

© editorial notes: Alun Wyn Bevan
© photographs: Huw Evans and all other individuals whose respective
  photographic contributions are acknowledged on page 160

This book is published with the financial support of the
Welsh Books Council

Printed and bound in Wales at
Gomer Press, Llandysul, Ceredigion

Contents

Introduction

For any sporting individual, the highest accolade awarded them is to represent their country. A few would push the boundary further and hope to do so with some aplomb – scoring a winning goal at the San Siro or Bernabeu, a sparkling century in front of a packed Lord's, or bringing the Millennium Stadium or Eden Park to its feet with a winning try.

An Olympic Gold was the challenge Lynn Davies set himself in the Tokyo Olympics of 1964, while for Ian Woosnam, the boyhood ambition was to sink that elusive putt in Augusta. For the rest of us, we can only imagine and admire the sense of achievement experienced by the likes of Colin Jackson, Nicole Cooke, Joe Calzaghe, Shane Williams, Ryan Giggs, Simon Jones, David Davies, and Geraint Thomas – all of whom have made it to the top and realised their goals.

If donning your country's vest or jersey is a feat accomplished by few, how much greater the honour if you are chosen as captain of a national team. Since the inception of the Welsh Rugby Union in 1887, only 127 players have held this position. What does it feel like to stand to attention as the national anthem is played, when the noise level from 80,000 passionate fans makes the most dispassionate observer feel a little tearful?

Whilst penning these few lines, I was struck by a bizarre coincidence. The first Welsh captain was a Mr A.J. Bevan, the latest Alun Wyn Jones, whilst yours truly is nominally a combination of both! You have to admit that there is a certain cachet attached to the title 'Captain' – in nautical terms we have the Captains James Cook, William Bligh, Christopher Columbus, Vasco de Gama. Children's authors have been quick to elevate a character by assigning him the title 'Captain' – think Haddock, Ahab, Hook, Pugwash, Hornblower, for example – not to mention the one and only Captain Mainwaring of *Dad's Army* fame! And there is a strong Welsh connection in the shape and form of Captain Henry Morgan, who plundered the Caribbean, and Robert Falcon Scott, the Antarctic explorer, who captained the *Terra Nova* which departed from Cardiff in 1910.

When I think back to my schooldays, one picture always comes to mind. Once we had decided on the sport of the day the next task was to select a team. The two best players would stand together, heads bowed, each making his selection. If you were any good, your name would be called almost immediately, and so it would proceed until there were two poor souls left standing whose enthusiasm greatly exceeded their ability!

These 'selectors' would always be captains and as such automatically qualify for a place in the team. This scenario may not always be the norm, however. An example is the former England test player Mike Brearley – he was not always the automatic choice as opening batsman for his country; in fact on some occasions he did not merit a place in the team. But his strength was his leadership; he was a master tactician and a man who could inspire his fellow teammates. 'I would have followed Martin Johnson through a brick wall,' remarked Scott Quinnell. 'But Martin would have shattered the brickwork prior to my arrival!'

Of the 127 captains who've skippered Wales at international level some became household names. Dickie Owen blazed on to the international scene in 1901 like a shooting star, bringing a new dimension to scrum-half play. Ever self-effacing, he stressed that his main responsibilty was to deliver a fast, accurate pass to his outside half, enabling him to set his backs in motion. He didn't captain Wales to victory over the 1905 All Blacks (their only defeat during their 36 match tour) but he was the pivot, playmaker, conductor, producer and director. He could have said, 'I didn't need to captain because I ran the show!' It was Owen who orchestrated proceedings and dictated the tactics on the day and started the move which led to Teddy Morgan's winning try. He captained Wales on three occasions.

Billy Trew led his country on 14 occasions, proving himself a shrewd tactician and a rousing and motivating leader. Out of Trew's 29 international appearances, Wales managed 23 victories; he also skippered Wales on 14 occasions, winning 12 of the matches played. Interestingly, Billy Trew captained Wales during the 1909 and 1911 Grand Slams but handed the captaincy to Johnnie Williams against France in 1911 because the Cardiff wing three-quarter spoke French!

Some captains have attained legendary status by virtue of the fact that they led the team to historic victories. Gwyn Nicholls was captain when Wales beat Dave Gallaher's 1905 All Blacks. Claude Davey repeated the feat in 1935 while Bleddyn Williams was the last Welsh captain to lead his team to victory against New Zealand in 1953.

There was a wait of almost a century before Wales beat South Africa – and what an occasion that turned out to be when the opening match at the new Millennium Stadium saw Robert Howley's men achieve an historic victory over the Springboks in 1999. While Wales have won the Championship and Triple Crown on many occasions there have been just ten Grand Slam winning captains. Brian Price came close in 1969, and but for the Troubles in Ireland in 1972 when the game was cancelled, John Lloyd could have had his name in the record books.

The 1970s are still referred to as the 'Golden Age' of Welsh Rugby and no one could argue with this description. Three Grand Slams in eight seasons – 1971, 1976 and 1978 – made household names of the respective captains, John Dawes, Mervyn Davies and Phil Bennett. The champagne and caviar days were to return again in 2005 and 2008 when Michael Owen, Gareth Thomas and Ryan Jones led the team to magnificent victories. The old Welsh style of playing exciting, flamboyant rugby was to prove successful once more.

There are other figures who merit a mention as influential captains – Richard Moriarty, who led Wales to third position in the Rugby World Cup in New Zealand in 1987; Ieuan Evans who led for 28 games during the 1990s when the national team was not at its best and struggled to keep up with the big boys of the Southern Hemisphere. Each and every rugby fan the length and breadth of Wales would, I am sure, be only too proud to emulate those 127 players who have led the national team over the years – we owe them a collective 'thank you' and 'well done'.

'We have a mountain to climb.' Words uttered by a succession of Welsh rugby captains since 1881 and words expressed by Welsh Rugby Union photographer Huw Evans when he realised his wife Sue (a non-smoker) was suffering from lung cancer in November 2008. The initial prognosis was not good, but Sue was determined not to yield. A large part of her treatment was carried out at Velindre Hospital, Cardiff, and it is to the staff there that the Evans family is indebted and wish to give heartfelt thanks for the part they played in Sue's present treatment and recovery.

Throughout his career, Huw's company has reacted positively to many fundraising ventures by providing photographs free of charge for various books, auctions etc. When the telephone call came from Velindre with a request for fundraising assistance, Huw leapt to the challenge with the aim of raising a massive one million pounds.

Together with Andrew Morris, the appointed Stepping Stones Fundraiser, Huw organised an assault on Mount Kilimanjaro, as fifteen former Welsh rugby captains agreed to 'reach for the stars'. And it's great to be able to say that Robert Howley, Scott Gibbs, Colin Charvis, Mark Taylor, Robert Jones, Ieuan Evans, Paul Thorburn, Bleddyn Bowen, Michael Owen, Andy Moore, Mike Hall, Eddie Butler, Robert Norster, Scott Quinnell and Jonathan Humphreys reached the summit. The appeal was launched at the Millennium Stadium in Cardiff during the summer of 2009 and received the full backing of the Welsh Rugby Union, including coach Warren Gatland. Donations can be sent to: Stepping Stones Appeal, Velindre Hospital, Whitchurch, Cardiff.

So why the book? Huw along with other agencies agreed to provide the pictures and I arranged to

subpoena the 61 former captains. The response from all concerned was so heartening – some returned emails, others responded by telephone, whilst a few, in handwriting which would have pleased the most experienced calligraphers, sent in their answers. I also had the opportunity to meet up with former icons of Welsh rugby – I shared two fantastic hours with John Gwilliam at his home in Llanfairfechan (Mrs Gwilliam's homemade lemonade a real treat), corresponded with the legendary Cliff Morgan, and lunched with Gerald Davies at the Nag's Head in Usk.

All profits will be donated to the Stepping Stones Appeal. All former captains refused any financial renumeration and gave freely of their time and efforts. Huw and I did not accept any financial rewards. We would like to thank Gomer Press, in particular Ceri Wyn Jones and Mairwen Prys Jones, for their guidance, help, patience and enthusiasm in formulating the publication.

Contacting the 61 Welsh rugby captains still alive was not an easy task, and my heartfelt thanks go out to all those who took the time and effort to reply. The cause is a deserving one. *Mae diolchiadau Huw a finnau yn gwbl ddiffuant.*

Alun Wyn Bevan
October 2010

9

'We have a mountain to climb.' These Captains Courageous climbed Kilimanjaro in September 2010 to raise funds for Velindre Hospital's Stepping Stones Appeal.
(Back row, l. to r.) Colin Charvis, Jonathan Humphreys, Warren Gatland, Bleddyn Bowen, Emyr Lewis, Andrew Moore, Sue Evans, Robert Norster, Eddie Butler, Mike Hall, Mark Taylor, Scott Quinnell, Paul Thorburn.
(Front row, l. to r.) Huw Evans, Garin Jenkins, Robert Jones, Ieuan Evans, Robert Howley.

Phil Bennett

He was a genius on a rugby field, whether it was for Llanelli at Stradey Park, for Wales at Cardiff, or for the Lions in Pretoria. And who can forget his role in Gareth Edwards's try for the Barbarians against the All Blacks in 1973. It was instigated out of sheer desperation when the maestro from Felinfoel, confronted by a desperate defensive situation, decided to attack! The rest, as they say, is history. Suffice to say that he is one of the best outside halves and footballers ever to have played the game.

Phil Bennett
on Daniel Carter

Q Which was your best match as captain?
A **Wales 16 France 7, March 18, 1978 (Cardiff). In
my final international appearance we defeated
a truly great French side who, like us, were
going for the Grand Slam. The atmosphere in the
capital city before, during and after the match
was simply electric. Gareth and I had decided
to retire at the final whistle and decided to
keep things quiet – we both felt that it was the
performance which mattered, not the halfbacks'
final farewell.**

Q Which was your finest hour as a rugby player?
A **(i) Llanelli 9 Seland Newydd 3, October 31, 1972
(Stradey Park), when I was one of the local
boys in a Scarlets team that beat the mighty All
Blacks.**

**(ii) South Africa 9 British Lions 26, July 13, 1974
(Port Elizabeth), when we clinched the Test
series, the first British Lions side to do so since
1896.**
**(iii) Winning the Llanelli School Sevens with
Coleshill Secondary Modern School, having
competed against teams such as Millfield,
Cowley Grammar and Bradford Grammar who
were legends of the seven-a-side game.**

Q Which current non-Welsh player would you love to
have in your team?
A **Daniel Carter (New Zealand)**

Q Who was the best captain you faced?
A **Graham Mourie (New Zealand) – a man of few
words.**

An iconic figure throughout the world of rugby.

Phil Bennett
on Shane Williams

14

Bleddyn Bowen

Profile

Bleddyn excelled in many sports but it is on the rugby field that he made the greatest impression. Whether playing for Swansea, South Wales Police or Wales, he was equally adept at outside half or in the centre. His ball-handling skills were exemplary, his dummy devastating, his left foot accurate and probing and he could control the game more by instinct than any pre-arranged plan. Indeed, several tries resulted from his quick vision in spotting a gap in the opposing defence. Though not physically imposing, he was the complete footballer.

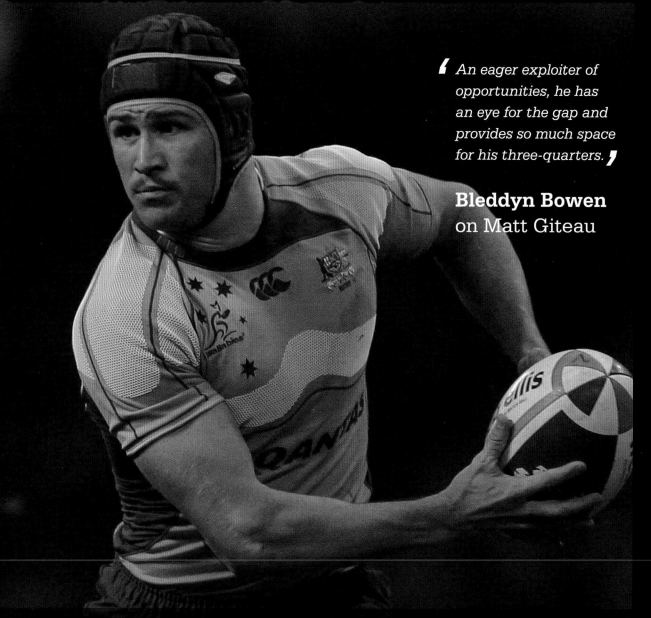

An eager exploiter of opportunities, he has an eye for the gap and provides so much space for his three-quarters.

Bleddyn Bowen
on Matt Giteau

Q Which was your best match as captain?
A Ireland 9 Wales 12, March 5, 1988 (Lansdowne Road). Wales won the Triple Crown for the first time in nine seasons thanks to Paul Thorburn's timely penalty goal in the dying minutes. Paul Moriarty claimed Wales's solitary try. It could and should have been a Grand Slam for Wales that year, but France beat us 10-9 at Cardiff.

Q Which was your finest hour as a rugby player?
A England vs Wales at Twickenham in 1986. Robert Jones and I, both from the village of Trebannws in the Swansea Valley and both former pupils at Cwmtawe Comprehensive School, ran out to face the old enemy. I managed to cross for a try, but Rob Andrew's seven penalty goals secured a narrow victory for England.

Q Which current Welsh player would you love to have in your team?
A Shane Williams, the Lionel Messi of world rugby!

Q Which current non-Welsh player would you love to have in your team?
A Matt Giteau (Australia)

Q Who was the best captain you faced?
A Wayne Shelford (New Zealand)

Q Who was the best captain you played under?
A Phil Noble (South Wales Police)

Onllwyn Brace

Profile

My father and grandfather were rugby fanatics and I distinctly remember them both singing the praises of Onllwyn Brace after seeing him displaying his skills for Newport and Wales in the 1950s. It was my privilege, however, at the 1960 Snelling Sevens at Cardiff Arms Park, to witness Onllwyn masterminding a magnificent Llanelli win ending Newport's dominance in the competition. He was outstanding: with his poise, panache, and penetration in evidence, I realise now that I was watching a rugby visionary.

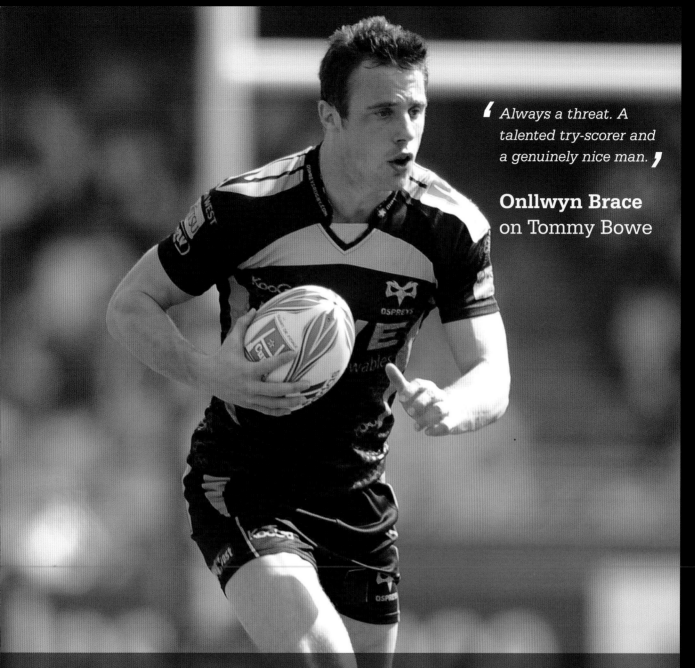

Always a threat. A talented try-scorer and a genuinely nice man.

Onllwyn Brace
on Tommy Bowe

Q   Which was your best match as captain?

A   **Ireland 9 Wales 10, March 12, 1960 (Lansdowne Road). A rare win in Dublin. Fullback Norman Morgan's conversion from the touchline ten minutes from time secured a dramatic victory.**

Q   Which was your finest hour as a rugby player?

A   **England 3 Wales 8 at Twickenham in 1956. My first cap, and with Cliff Morgan as my halfback partner.**

Q   Who would be the first name on your team sheet?

A   **J.P.R. Williams**

Q   Which current Welsh player would you love to have in your team?

A   **Shane Williams. Small of stature but big of heart, he is the true embodiment of Welsh rugby – talented, innovative and enterprising.**

Q   Which current non-Welsh player would you love to have in your team?

A   **Tommy Bowe**

Q   Who was the best captain you faced?

A   **Bob Stuart (New Zealand) at Rodney Parade, Newport, in 1953.**

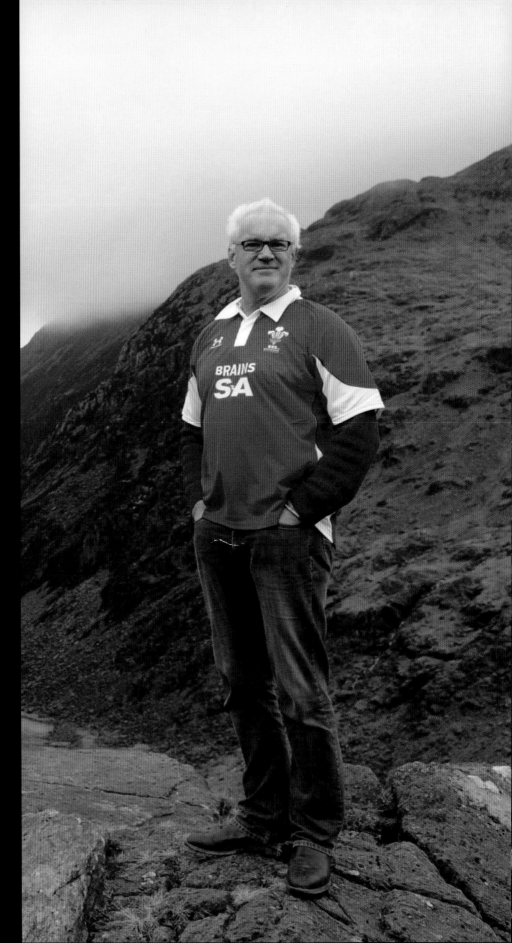

Eddie Butler

Profile

For over 25 years, the former Pontypool, Cambridge University, Wales and British Lions No.8 forward has been a regular columnist with *The Observer* newspaper and an eloquently astute commentator on BBC television. Though he came from an academic background, the gifted linguist felt more at home at Pontypool Park than he did on the manicured lawns of King's College. A very underrated player, he contributed greatly to Pooler's glory days when his hero and mentor was the former bulldozer driver and former Wales and British Lions front-row forward Ray Prosser.

> *He supplies the line-out ball that starts the process of moving play forward.*

Eddie Butler
on Victor Matfield

Q Which was your best match as captain?

A **Scotland 15 Wales 19, February 19, 1983 (Murrayfield). We went on the field fifteen angry men after the criticism received after the 13-13 draw against England at Cardiff Arms Park. Staff Jones, scored a debut try, and Elgan Rees raced over after a typical Clive Rees forage on the left-hand side. All in all it was a very professional performance; Murrayfield hasn't been a happy hunting ground for Wales over the years!**

Q Which was your finest hour as a rugby player?

A **(i) That elusive first cap against France at the Arms Park in 1980, when, as a fluent French speaker, I could actually interpret all the line-out calls!**

(ii) Pontypool's Schweppes Cup Final win against Swansea in 1983.
(iii) The 24 points we scored against England in 1984, the most scored at Twickenham since the ground's opening in 1910. I even had a hand in Adrian Hadley's try after Bleddyn Bowen's break and dummy.

Q Which current non-Welsh player would you love to have in your team?

A **Victor Matfield**

Q Who was the best captain you faced?

A **Andrew Slack (Australia) in 1984.**

Q Who was the best player to captain?

A **David Bishop – challenging, unconventional, but a genius.**

Colin Charvis

Profile

From the very outset Colin proved himself to be an outstanding back-row forward and crowd favourite. Physically he was a giant of a man – tall, athletically-built, possessing poweful, muscular arms. That robust physique made him a difficult adversary in all phases of the game and an immense presence at rucks and mauls. In the maul, it was an experience to see him wrenching the ball away from opposing forwards before releasing it into the safe hands of the waiting scrum half. Colin's ability to offload a telling pass just as he was about to go to ground also proved highly effective.

' The best captain
I faced. '

**Colin Charvis
on Jon Smit**

Q Which was your best match as captain?
A Wales 37 New Zealand 53, November 2, 2003
   (Sydney). Let's be honest, we gave the All Blacks
   a scare in this magnificent Rugby World Cup
   pool match. At the start of the second half we
   even led by 37-33 with several players, who
   hadn't featured previously, proving their mettle
   in a titanic contest. We lost, but I was a proud
   captain.

Q Which was your finest hour as a rugby player?
A (i) Wales 32 England 31, April 11, 1999
   (Wembley). 'Our chances are pretty remote,'
   remarked coach Graham Henry and most of our
   supporters would have agreed. But in the second
   minute of injury time the inimitable Scott Gibbs
   danced his way to the try line, before Neil
   Jenkins's conversion sealed the victory. Graham

Henry added, 'Neil Jenkins is the best goal-
kicker I've ever worked with. And I've worked
with Grant Fox!'
(ii) Wales 29 South Africa 19, June 26, 1999
(Cardiff). At the then unfinished Millennium
Stadium, defeating the Springboks for the first
time ever was particularly pleasing for me
personally as I'd played in the 'lambs to the
slaughter' annihilation at Pretoria in June 1998.

Q Who would be the first name on your team
   sheet?
A Garin Jenkins

Q Which opponent did you respect the most?
A Richard Hill (England)

Q Who was the best captain you played under?
A Anthony Clement (Swansea)

Colin Charvis's primal scream against Argentina during the 1999 World Cup.

Terry Cobner

Profile

Terry Cobner was an inspirational wing forward whose strength and speed around the field was legendary. This, coupled with his resilience and stamina, made him a formidable opponent. Cobner's style of play is what the modern-day player aspires to, and his ability to change the tempo of a movement in an instant led to opportunities for others. On the field the Pontypool dynamo could be seen either charging around making bone-crunching tackles or creating effective platforms from which his fellow players could create attacking moves.

The best Welsh tight-head prop I saw or played with.

Terry Cobner
on Graham Price

Q Which was your first match as captain?

A **Wales 20 Argentina 19, October 16, 1976 (Cardiff). No caps were awarded but every one of us deserved some form of recognition as it proved to be a titanic struggle. We eventually squeezed home thanks to a last-minute penalty goal kicked by Phil Bennett after Travaglini's dangerous tackle on JPR.**

Q Which was your finest hour as a rugby player?

A **(i) My work with the British Lions forwards during the tour of New Zealand in 1977. For once the Lions forwards outplayed their opponents. (ii) Ten years as captain of Pontypool RFC. From the bottom of the pile, we became one of the best club sides in the United Kingdom.**

(iii) Scoring the winning try for Wales on my international debut against Scotland on January 19, 1974. Gerald had been tackled yards short of the try line but somehow managed to flick the ball backwards to a supporting player. I happened to be there; the try proved crucial in a 6-0 victory.

Q Who was your childhood rugby hero?

A **Colin Evans – scrum half for Blaenavon Forgeside before he went on to Pontypool, Newport, Wales (1 cap against England at Twickenham in 1960) and then Keighley Rugby League Football Club.**

Q Who was the best captain you played under?

A **Mike Davies of the Staffordshire team which won the County Championship in 1970.**

Gareth Davies

Profile

Gareth Davies won the first of his 21 caps at Ballymore in Brisbane in 1978 and established himself as first choice for Cardiff and Wales for several seasons, leading to his selection for the British Lions tour of South Africa in 1980. With all the attributes of a great outside half, he was also one of the best kickers of his generation. Indeed, as Gwyn Prescott declares in *Cardiff Sporting Greats*, 'Had Brian McKechnie missed a highly controversial penalty in the dying moments of the game against the 1978 All Blacks, Gareth would have been immortalised alongside the Welsh victors over New Zealand of earlier generations.'

Both creative and destructive as a flanker, he has been pound for pound the best rugby player in the world during the past five years.

Gareth Davies
on Richie McCaw

Q Which was your best match as captain?
A **Wales 18 Australia 13, December 5, 1981 (Cardiff). My very first game in charge was a splendid contest which saw Richard Moriarty plunge over for a debut try, the only try scored against the 1981/82 Wallabies in seven matches in Wales.**

Q Which was your finest hour as a rugby player?
A **There were so many. The finest were the ones immediately after a great win, with your teammates in the inner sanctum of the private dressing rooms when emotions were high.**

Q Who was the first name on your team sheet?
A **Terry Holmes**

Q Which current Welsh player would you love to have in your team?
A **Shane Williams. With him, the game is never lost.**

Q Which current non-Welsh player would you love to have in your team?
A **Richie McCaw**

Q Who was the best captain you faced?
A **Jean-Pierre Rives**

Q Who was the best captain you played under?
A **Dave Smyth of the UWIST team which won the UAU Championship in 1976, the first Welsh University to accomplish the feat. Dave played for Ballymena and Ulster.**

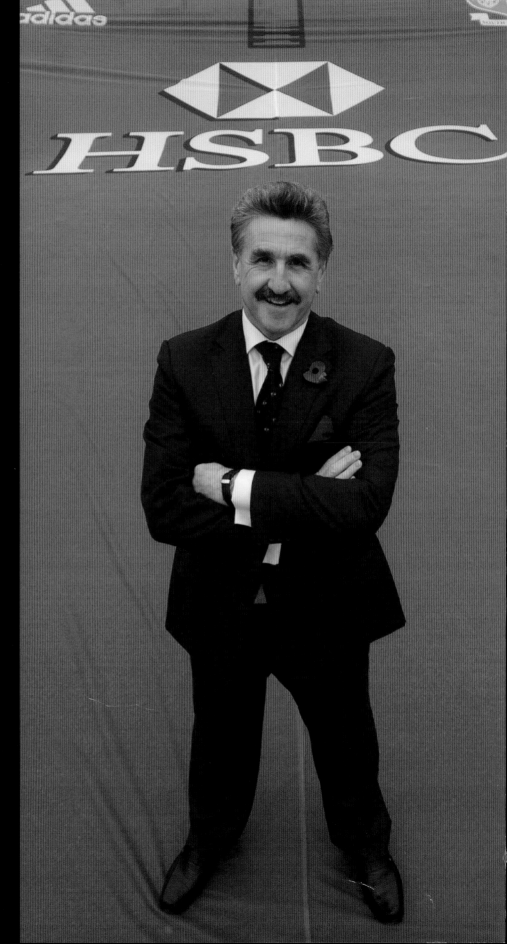

Gerald Davies

Profile

There are those whose sporting prowess on the field is matched by their flamboyant personality off it – in fact, the latter often competes for column inches with the former. Not so with Gerald Davies from the village of Llansaint in Carmarthenshire. A reserved, modest individual, who always let his rugby do the talking, Gerald was revered by players, fans and the media alike. Indeed, there is never any debate about who was the best right wing three-quarter ever. It is always T.G.R. Davies. He will always be remembered as a quite extraordinary rugby player on the field, and a true ambassador and gentleman off it.

Q Which was your first match as captain?
A Wales 26 Tonga 7, October 19, 1974 (Cardiff).
It had always been a dream of mine to lead
Wales onto the hallowed turf at the Arms
Park, proudly wearing our traditional red
jerseys. And though no caps were awarded,
it was still a privilege and honour to
captain one's country. You can imagine my
disappointment, however, when I realised
that Wales, for the very first time in their
history, would not be wearing red but green!

Q Which was your finest hour as a rugby player?
A (i) Wales 11 Australia 14, December 3, 1966
(Cardiff). My first cap but I must admit I
remember very little about the occasion
apart from the fact that it heralded
international debuts for Barry John, Delme
Thomas, Keith Braddock and myself.
(ii) The 1971 Grand Slam matches. I was also

involved in the 1976 and 1978 campaigns
but there's always something rather special
about accomplishing something for the first
time.
(iii) New Zealand 14 British Lions 14, August
14, 1971 (Eden Park, Auckland). Though this
fourth test was drawn, it was still enough to
clinch the series for us.
(iv) The four tries I scored against the
mighty Pontypool at Pontypool Park in the
Schweppes Cup in 1978. Not, I stress, for
any personal satisfaction but from an overall
team perspective on an occasion when the
confidence and self-assurance was infectious.

Q Who were your schoolboy rugby heroes?
A Carwyn James and Cliff Morgan.

Q Which current non-Welsh players would you
love to have in your team?
A Imanol Harinordoquy and Brian O'Driscoll.

GERALD DAVIES Q&A

Carwyn James in thoughtful
mood with the Lions in 1971.

Brian O'Driscoll celebrates the Irish Grand Slam in 2009.

Jonathan Davies

Profile

Players like Jonathan aren't born every day! There is something in their genetic make-up that sets them apart. There are those at the Gnoll who still talk about the try he scored against the English champions, Bath. The game had been a hotly-contested affair with the result in the balance until Jonathan received possession from a centre-field scrum. He feigned a drop-goal attempt, and then like a bullet sped past five if not six Bath defenders who resembled the proverbial rabbits caught in the headlights of a car. The headlines the following day read 'Genius, destroyer, showman'.

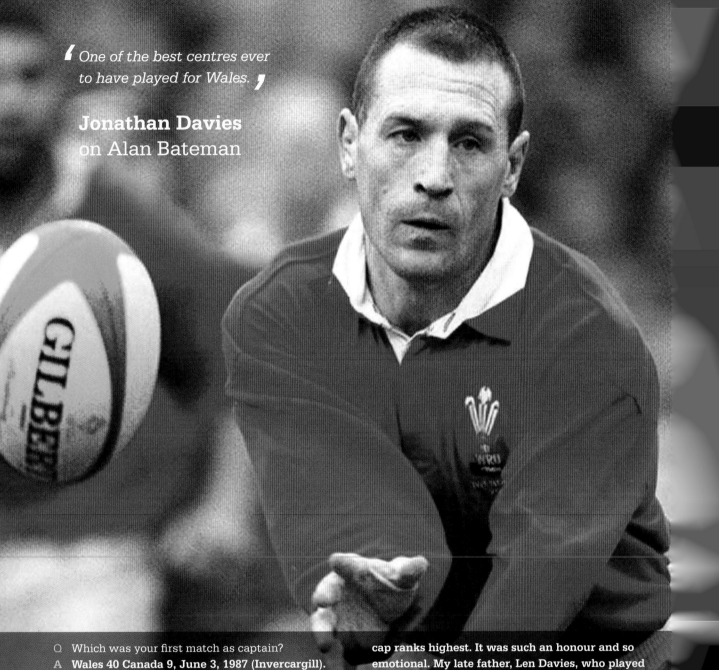

> 'One of the best centres ever to have played for Wales.'

Jonathan Davies
on Alan Bateman

Q   Which was your first match as captain?
A   **Wales 40 Canada 9, June 3, 1987 (Invercargill). Although Richard Moriarty, the official World Cup captain came off the bench to replace his brother Paul, I continued to captain the team. I was partnered at halfback by Aberavon's Ray Giles, and will-o'-the-wisp wing Ieuan Evans helped himself to four tries.**

Q   Which was your finest hour as a rugby player?
A   **Wales 24 England 15, April 20, 1985 (Cardiff). The try against Australia for Great Britain at Wembley would have been a highlight for many Rugby League fans, but on a personal level the honour of winning my first Welsh**

cap ranks highest. It was such an honour and so emotional. My late father, Len Davies, who played for Swansea in the 1950s, would have been so proud, especially as I crossed for a try and dropped a goal.

Q   Which current Welsh player would you love to have in your team?
A   **Shane Williams. People just stare in disbelief at some of his efforts. Magic!**

Q   Which current non-Welsh player would you love to have in your team?
A   **Daniel Carter. A prodigious talent. Quite simply the best outside half in world rugby.**

'The first name on my team sheet.'

Jonathan Davies
on Terry Holmes

Mefin Davies

Profile

Mefin was a hooker from the time he could crawl. If medals were awarded for grit, determination, ability and a never-say-die attitude, then the front-row forward from Nantgaredig in Carmarthenshire would be the first recipient. Badly let down by individuals and regions when the Celtic Warriors tragically disbanded, he was one of the few players sidelined by David Moffet's cull. But Mefin fought back. He became a cult hero at Gloucester and Leicester, two outstanding Guinness Premiership sides, and eventually displaced three international hookers in Olivier Azam, Benjamin Kayser, and George Chuter.

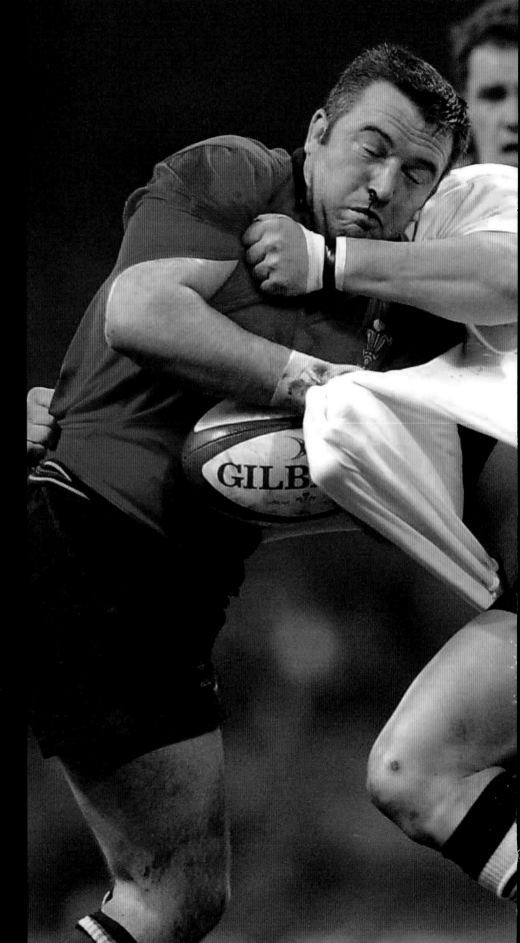

A master at manipulating the referee.

Mefin Davies
on Lawrence Dallaglio

Q   Which was your best match as captain?
A   **Wales 54 Romania 8, August 27, 2003 (Racecourse Ground, Wrexham). It was my only game as captain! It was the match which clinched Shane Williams's place as third-choice scrum half for the 2003 Rugby World Cup.**

Q   Which was your finest hour as a rugby player?
A   **South Africa 34 Wales 19, June 8, 2002 (Bloemfontein). This was my first cap, and only just beats being part of the Grand Slam squad in 2005.**

Q   What's your motto?
A   **Work hard, play hard.**

Q   Who would be the first name on your team sheet?
A   **Adam Jones – to make sure the scrum is in order.**

Q   Which current Welsh player would you love to have in your team?
A   **Shane Williams. He has the ability to create magic on the field.**

Q   Which current non-Welsh player would you love to have in your team?
A   **Richie McCaw. The world's best open-side flanker.**

Q   Who was the best captain you faced?
A   **Lawrence Dallaglio**

Mervyn Davies

Profile

A talisman of the great London Welsh teams of the 1960s and 1970s, Merve the Swerve became one of the most iconic of Welsh captains, with his trademark headband and thick moustache. A Grand Slam winner in 1971, he established an international reputation for himself as a No.8 forward on the 1971 and 1974 Lions tours, before he led Wales to another Grand Slam in 1976. A life-threatening injury sustained whilst playing for Swansea that year denied him further glory, but he continued to be regarded as one of the all-time great No. 8 forwards.

> *The first name on my team sheet.*

Mervyn Davies
on Gerald Davies

Q Which was your first match as captain?
A France 10 Wales 25, January 18, 1975 (Parc des Princes, Paris). Our record in Paris was a dismal one and we fielded six new caps. It was a pleasure and a privilege to captain a side that scored five outstanding tries.

Q Which was your best match as captain?
A Wales 19 France 13, March 6, 1976 (Cardiff). This brought another Grand Slam triumph for Wales. J.J. Williams scored our solitary try with Phil Bennett, Steve Fenwick and Allan Martin kicking vital penalty goals. The match remained very much in the balance up to the very last minute when JPR's shoulder tackle prevented Jean-François Gourdon from scoring in the corner. I was in some pain throughout having been kicked in the calf in the opening exchanges.

Q Which was your finest hour as a rugby player?
A Being alive after the the 1971 First Test against New Zealand at Dunedin! We were absolutely smashed, pulverised even . . . but we came off the field, looked at the scoreboard and realised we'd won 9-3. I still can't believe it!

Q Which current Welsh player would you love to have in your team?
A Gethin Jenkins

Q Which current non-Welsh player would you love to have in your team?
A Richie McCaw. He knows the off-side law!

Q Who was the best captain you faced?
A Jacques Fouroux

Q Who was the best captain you played under?
A John Dawes

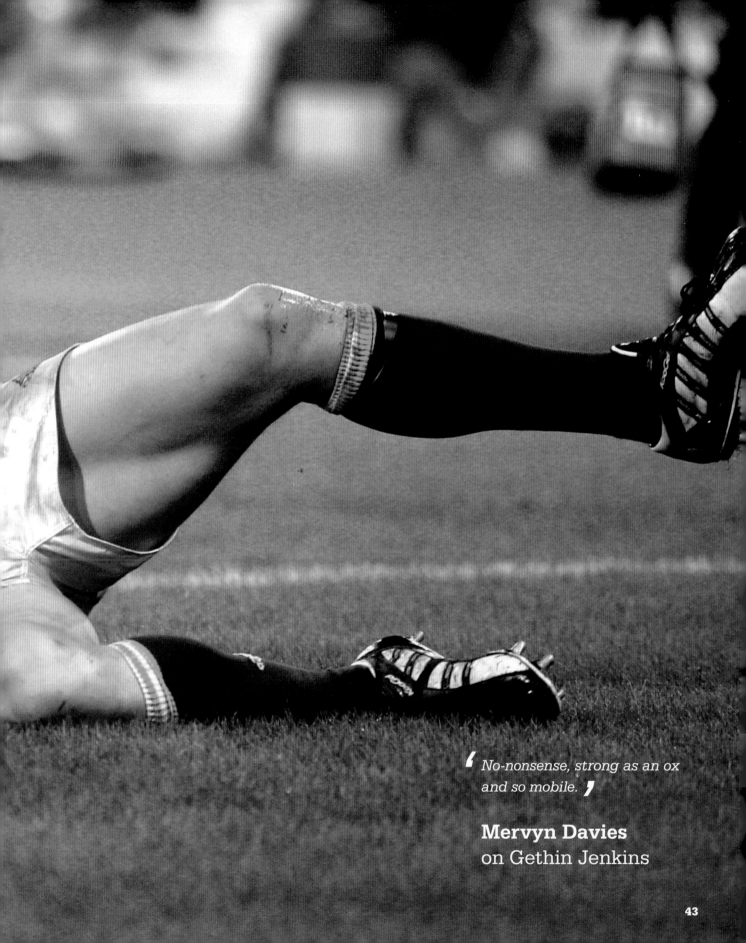

‘ *No-nonsense, strong as an ox and so mobile.* ’

Mervyn Davies
on Gethin Jenkins

Nigel Davies

Profile

Llanelli's Nigel Davies exhibited deft skills with the ball in hand. His ability to hypnotise defences, create space (where by right there should be none) and maintain a cool head in the heat of battle often left spectators breathless. He had that touch of nonchalant wizardry which allowed him to deceive and totally bemuse the opposition. Even when tackled he somehow managed to release a perfect pass into the waiting hands of a supporting runner. His only match as captain of Wales was a floodlit fixture against France at the National Stadium in 1996. It proved a sorry affair for Nigel: he dislocated his ankle after 25 minutes!

My schoolboy hero.

Nigel Davies
on Ray Gravell

Terry Davies

Profile

Terry Davies was one of the outstanding personalities of the successful British Lions tour to New Zealand in 1959 and according to the local aficionados was one of the most impressive players in the visitors' line-up. He was accorded regular complimentary column inches in the country's rugby-centred newspapers, and along with second-row forward Rhys Haydn Williams, was the player New Zealanders wanted most to have in their ranks. Praise indeed! What's more, his knack of initiating incisive counter-attacks out of defence would have made him equally successful in today's professional game.

Two very promising Welsh youngsters.

Terry Davies on Jason Tovey (above)
and Tavis Knoyle (below)

John
Dawes

Profile

Though John Dawes may not have been able to compete with Bleddyn Williams, Brian O'Driscoll, Philippe Sella and Jeremy Guscott in terms of individual flair and raw pace, any would-be selectors of an all-time dream XV would have to weigh up other qualities John had to offer. John was a catalyst both in attack and defence, and undoubtedly one of sport's great captains in the Mike Brearley, Clive Lloyd, Franz Beckenbauer and Steve Waugh mould. He is the only player from Britain to have captained the British Lions to a series win in New Zealand.

Q   Which was your first match as captain?

A   **Ireland 9 Wales 6, March 9, 1968 (Lansdowne Road). An eventful match deservedly won by Tom Kiernan's XV by 9-6. Irate spectators invaded the field when referee Mike Titcomb awarded a dropped goal to Gareth Edwards even though the ball clearly drifted wide of the post.**

Q   Which was your best match as captain?

A   **Barbarians 17 New Zealand 11, January 27, 1973 (Cardiff). Cliff Morgan's commentary, describing the greatest try ever scored, has gone down in history: 'Kirkpatrick to Williams. This is great stuff! Phil Bennett covering chased by Alistair Scown. Brilliant! Oh, that's brilliant! John Williams, Bryan Williams, Pullin. John Dawes, great dummy. To David,**

Tom David . . . the halfway line! Brilliant by Quinnell! This is Gareth Edwards! A dramatic start! What a score!!!'

Q   Which was your finest hour as a rugby player?

A   **New Zealand 14 British Lions 14, July 14, 1971 (Eden Park, Auckland). Referee John Pring's final whistle at the end of the Fourth Test Match signalled a 2-1 series victory, which still remains the sole Lions success in New Zealand.**

Q   Who would be the first name on your team sheet?

A   **Gerald Davies**

Q   Which current Welsh player would you love to have in your team?

A   **Shane Williams**

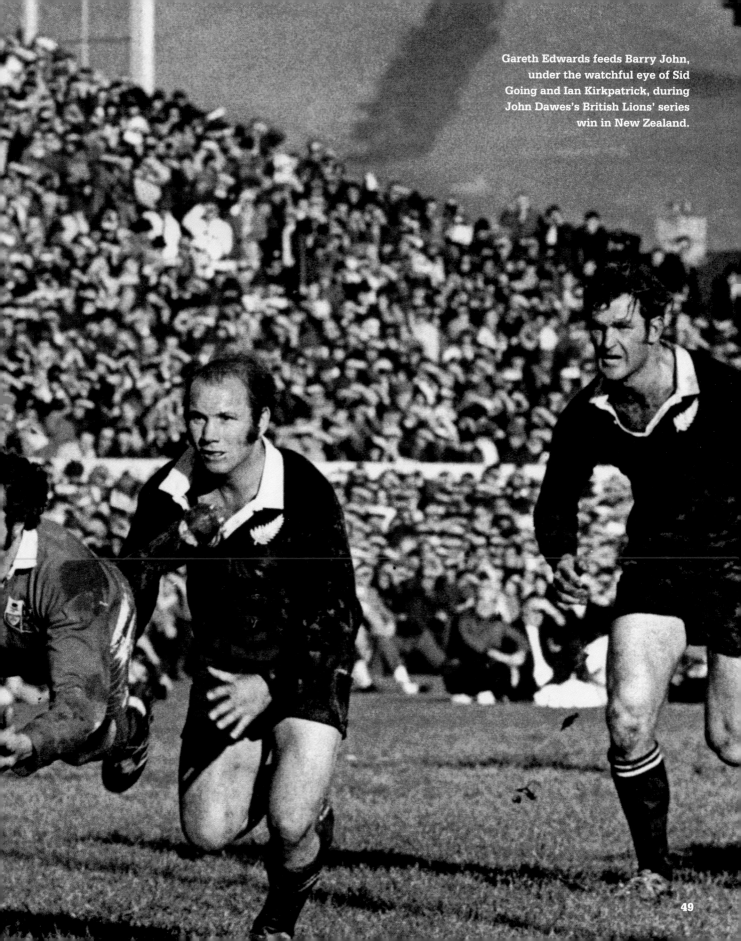

Gareth Edwards feeds Barry John, under the watchful eye of Sid Going and Ian Kirkpatrick, during John Dawes's British Lions' series win in New Zealand.

Gareth Edwards

Profile

In these days of professional rugby, I wonder whether there is enough money to finance the franchise that could put on the field the fifteen best players ever to have played the game? One thing I do know, however, is that there would be no shortage of armchair selectors eager to select such a team – and they wouldn't have to invest a single penny! And while there would be fierce debate over fourteen of the positions, there would be no contest when it came to choosing the scrum half. The No. 9 shirt would automatically go to Gareth Owen Edwards of Gwaun-cae-gurwen.

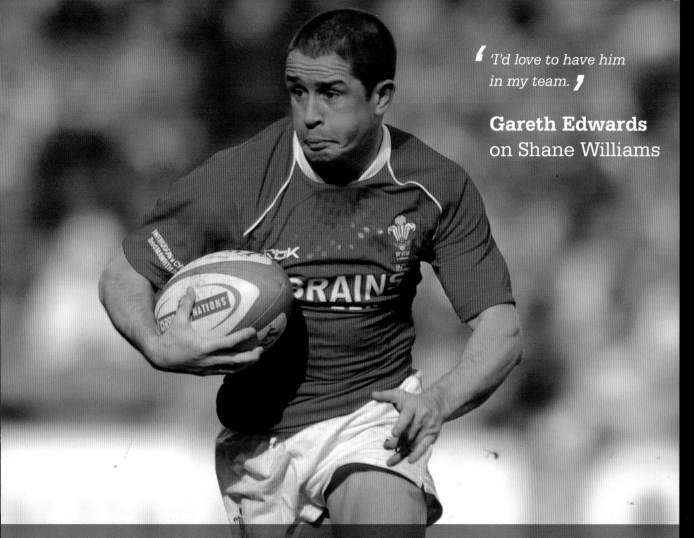

Gareth Edwards
on Shane Williams

Q Which was your best match as captain?

A (i) Wales 30 England 9, April 12, 1969 (Cardiff). The mercurial Maurice Richards crossed for four tries equalling Willie Llewellyn and Reggie Gibbs's record. Barry John scored our fifth try, a breathtaking effort which has been replayed on numerous occasions since. It was Wales's 11th Triple Crown title.

(ii) East Wales 3 New Zealand 3, December 9, 1967 (Cardiff). The 1967 New Zealand All Blacks were described as the world's best. And on their tour of Britain, France and Canada, they won 16 of their 17 games; the only team they failed to beat was East Wales. Coach Dai Hayward and I as captain sorted out our tactics in the Cockney Pride Tavern in Cardiff. Over a curry and a pint of Brains, Dai came up with a winning formula: 'Gareth, we're going to tackle everything in black, and win all the loose possession. Then we're going to run with the ball and cause chaos. Easy!' We deserved to win and even the All Blacks manager, Charlie Sexton, admitted in the post-match function, 'We were second best!'

Q Which was your finest hour as a rugby player?

A (i) New Zealand 14 British Lions 14, July 14, 1971 (Eden Park, Auckland). The draw enabled us to win a Test series in New Zealand for the very first time – we still haven't repeated the feat.

(ii) That Barbarians try! Phil started it all near his own goal line, others contributed (JPR, John Pullin, John Dawes, Derek, and Tom David) and I managed to finish it off with a dramatic dive in the corner.

(iii) Achieving three Grand Slams in 1971, 1976 and 1978 under the respective captaincies of John Dawes, Mervyn Davies and Phil Bennett. J.P.R. Williams and I had the honour and added distinction of playing in all three Slams, a total of twelve matches. Gerald played in eleven, but missed out through injury on the France match in 1978.

He was the opponent that I respected above all others.

Gareth Edwards
on Sid Going

Ieuan Evans

Profile

In a glittering career, Ieuan won 72 caps and scored 33 tries. As captain on 28 occasions, Ieuan refused to capitulate in the face of some stern criticism from the press, commentators and public alike, and was always most supportive of his players, never failing to encourage them. He instilled in his team a sense of pride which bore fruit on that day in Cardiff on February 6, 1993 when they faced mighty England. It may have been Emyr Lewis's kick that began the move but it was Ieuan's lightning speed and his ability to control the ball that brought the try and with it a magnificent victory.

Ieuan Evans
on Sean Fitzpatrick

Q Which was your first match as captain?
A **Wales 9 France 22, September 4, 1991 (Cardiff). This was the very first floodlit international played at the National Stadium. Alan Davies was caretaker coach, and team manager Bob Norster had to be introduced to him!**

Q Which was your finest hour as an international rugby player?
A **(i) France 16 Wales 9, February 7, 1987 (Parc des Princes, Paris). My first cap!**
(ii) Being part of the successful British Lions Test team in Australia in 1989. In a physically-demanding series, I had managed to keep David Campese quiet, and was on hand to pounce for a try when he counter-attacked unsuccessfully from behind his own goal line in the final Test.

(iii) The 1993 Lions series in New Zealand. I played some of my best rugby on that tour, and but for some indifferent refereeing in the first test match at Christchurch, we could well have won the series. One decision in that match still rankles – I caught a high kick from Grant Fox, fell over the goal line, still holding on to the ball, with Frank Bunce in close attendance. Imagine my horror when, from a long way off, the referee awarded a try. Television cameras confirmed that the try should never have been awarded.

Q Who was the best captain you faced?
A **Sean Fitzpatrick**

Q Who was the best captain you played under?
A **Finlay Calder**

' *One of the best wingers ever.* '

Ieuan Evans
on David Campese

Steve Fenwick

Profile

If the Bridgend, Wales and British Lions centre three-quarter were playing today, all the clubs in Europe would be bidding extravagantly for his services. Steve was a playmaker, a sensor of opportunities, and an exploiter of opponents' hesitancy. Though built like an ox, he had the light-footed finesse of the ballet dancer. And with a chess grandmaster's overview of what was happening around him, his choice of running angles was often devastating. He formed a superb centre partnership with the legendary Ray Gravell, before going on to distinguish himself as a professional rugby league player.

A centre after my own heart!

Steve Fenwick
on Yannick Jauzion

Scott Gibbs

Profile

Scott represented Wales and Great Britain in both codes of rugby. However, a juggled ball, three sidesteps and a single-handed salute while crossing the whitewash at Wembley Stadium will almost certainly be his legacy. Everyone can remember where they were when it happened, which may be both an indication of the grandeur of Gibbs's achievement, as well as how ridiculously seriously we Welsh take our national game. And who can forget his hand-off during the 1997 Lions tour of South Africa when he single-handedly knocked the Springbok front row, in the shape of Os du Randt, off their mythical pedestal!

❝ A great player and leader. ❞

Scott Gibbs
on Martin Johnson

John Gwilliam

Profile

David Parry-Jones's enthralling overview of Welsh rugby in the early 1950s, *The Gwilliam Seasons* (Seren, 2002), encapsulates a golden era, and pays tribute to the double Grand Slam winning captain: 'Gwilliam . . . left Wales to serve in the army during the Second World War and took teaching posts in Scotland and England during his working life. Consequently he seldom played in Wales, and was not part of the close rugby scene of inter-club rivalry and politicking . . . As a player he was an athletic and technically gifted forward, but also a deep thinker about the game, who liked to produce the unexpected.'

The mercurial Cliff Morgan, one of the stars of John Gwilliam's Welsh teams.

Q Which was your first match as captain?
A England 5 Wales 11, January 20, 1950 (Twickenham). The previous day at Herne Hill a senior official of the Welsh Rugby Union came to me and said, 'Unfortunately, Bleddyn cannot play, Rees Stephens the vice-captain is also injured, so we are making you captain tomorrow. You are quite free to play your own game, but don't hold the ball in the back row of the scrum, don't throw out any of those long passes and don't flip the ball back from the line-out.'

Q Who would have been the first names on your team sheet?
A Cliff Morgan and Ken Jones were two outstanding individuals. Cliff was mercurial and I remember him creating magnificent tries for Ken Jones at Twickenham and Lansdowne Road during our 1952 Grand Slam Season. Ken was a sporting all-rounder and I distinctly remember travelling down from Cambridge to watch him compete for Great Britain in the 1948 Olympic Games. It was a very special day with Ken receiving a Silver Medal in the 4 x 100 metre relay. It really was an 'I was there' moment.

Q Which opposing captain made the most impression?
A Karl Mullen (Ireland)

Q Who were your most respected opponents?
A South Africa in 1950.

Q Who was the best captain you played under?
A Haydn Tanner

He has the ability and temperament to become a truly great player.

John Gwilliam
on James Hook

Mike
Hall

Profile

Throughout his career with Maesteg, Bridgend, Cardiff, Cambridge University, Wales and the British Lions, Mike was an outstanding competitor whose attacking qualities proved successful against the most organised of defences. He was also a ferocious tackler who time and again proved himself a vital cog in well-oiled back divisions for club and country. Since retitrement he has proved himself to be a knowledgeable and highly intelligent broadcaster on BBC Television's *Scrum V*, as well as becoming a highly successful businessman.

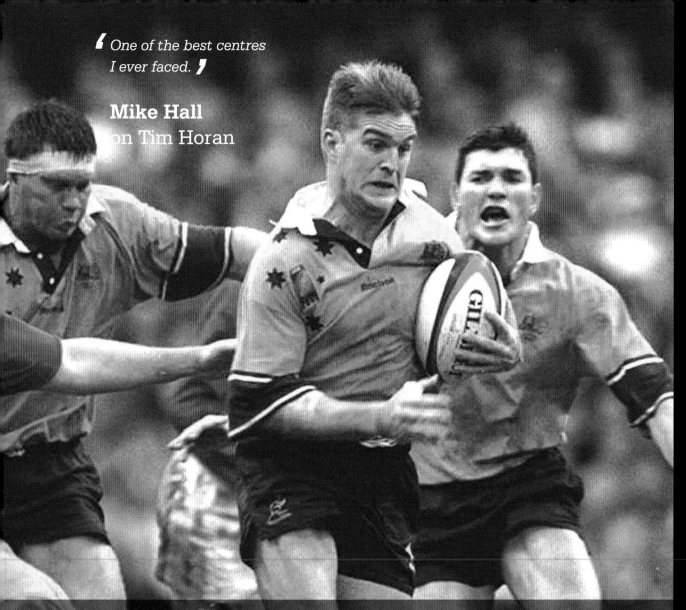

Mike Hall
on Tim Horan

Q Which was your first match as captain?

A **Wales 9 New Zealand 34, May 31, 1995 (Ellis Park, Johannesburg). I summed up our performance at the final whistle with the following, 'We were all like rabbits caught in the headlights.'**

Q Which was your finest hour as a rugby player?

A **(i) Wales 12 England 9, March 18, 1989 (Cardiff). Victory for the old enemy would have given them the Championship, but we never gave in and just deserved to win by 12-9. When Rory Underwood's pass to Jon Webb went astray, I just slid and hoped for the best. I must admit it was a little dubious; I was as surprised as anyone but referee Kerry Fitzgerald, who controlled the Rugby World Cup final in 1987, was in no doubt and awarded the try.**

**(ii) Representing the British Lions was a great honour. I was a member of Finlay Calder's 1989 team, where I partnered Brendan Mullin in the First Test defeat at Sydney.
(iii) Captaining Cardiff to victory over Llanelli in the 1994 Swalec Cup Final was a great personal milestone.**

Q Which current Welsh player would you love to have in your team?

A **James Hook**

Q Which current non-Welsh player would you love to have in your team?

A **Pierre Spies (South Africa)**

Terry Holmes

Profile

The role of scrum half in a team whose forwards are dominant can be relatively straightforward. But that luxury was rarely afforded to Terry Holmes during his tenure as national scrum half in the 1980s. However, when Wales was able to scrape together the occasional victory, or when the blow of an overwhelming defeat was temporarily lessened, it was usually thanks to his superhuman exploits. He was a giant amongst scrum halves, and in a list of world class Welsh No. 9s (starting with Dickie Owen and ending with Mike Phillips and Dwayne Peel) Terry Holmes would be in there with the best of them.

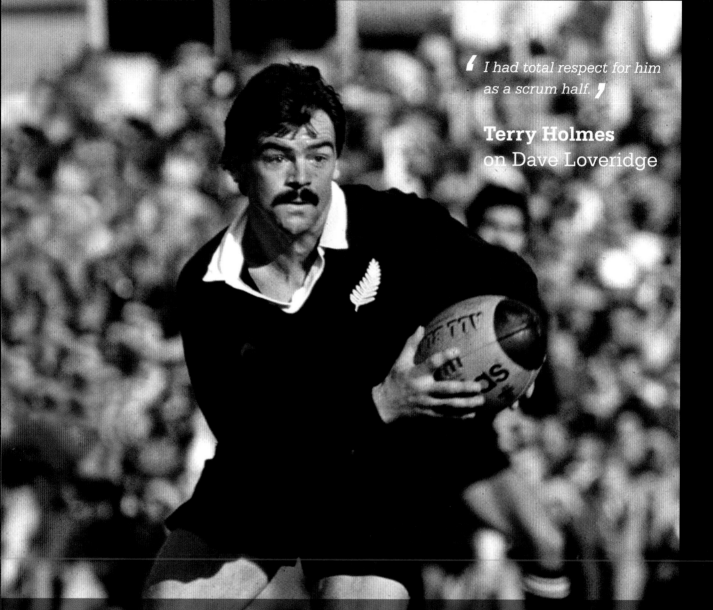

Q   Which was your first match as captain?

A   **Scotland 21 Wales 25, March 2, 1985
    (Murrayfield). I'd always had a good record
    against Scotland (played 4; won 4) and this
    I suppose was the icing on the cake. Gareth
    Davies was recalled and dropped a goal after
    50 seconds to calm the nerves – pack leader
    David Pickering was in impressive form, and
    crossed for two tries.**

Q   Which was your finest hour as a rugby player?

A   **(i) Wales 27 England 3, March 17, 1979
    (Cardiff). There was always something rather
    special about defeating the old enemy. Mike
    Roberts was recalled and described by John
    Billot as the Edward G Robinson of the Welsh
    pack. He might have been grey and elderly**
    but he scored from close range and inspired us to
    score 14 points in nine glorious minutes. JPR left
    the field to have stitches inserted in a leg wound
    providing Clive Griffiths with a first cap, and he
    set up a final try for Elgan Rees. We'd won the
    Triple Crown for a fourth consecutive season.
    (ii) I still have nightmares about that New
    Zealand match in 1978. I won't bore you with all
    the details but we had them on the ropes. Then
    New Zealand, of all teams, resorted to shoddy
    tactics to win a match – a deliberate dive out of
    the line-out, the referee took the bait and the rest
    is history!
    (iii) Beating Bridgend 14-6 in the 1981 Schweppes
    Cup Final made for a very special day (and
    night!).

Robert Howley

Who can forget Robert Howley's scintillating debut try against England at Twickenham in 1996, making a mockery of the claim that England's defence was impregnable. His 75-metre sprint for the line at the Stade de France in 1999 was heroic and resulted in a shock 34-33 win for the men in red. 'Pay back time,' remarked skipper Howley after the 51-0 defeat at Wembley a year earlier! Another spectacular try two years later at the Stade de France was described by John Billot in the 2001-02 edition of Rugby Annual for Wales as worthy of Harry Potter's Wronski Feint!

Q Which was your finest hour as a rugby player?

A (i) I had always wanted to win my first cap in the Five Nations as opposed to against a touring team or in a friendly international. Against England at Twickenham on February 3, 1996, one of my boyhood dreams came true.

(ii) Wales's ten consecutive victories during the1998/99 and 1999/2000 seasons, including the legendary triumph at Wembley as England were left in a state of bewilderment after Scott and Neil's last-gasp efforts.

(iii) Captaining Wales to their first and, as yet, only victory against the Springboks.

(iv) I heard the news of my Lions selection in 1997 from a Sky Sports reporter a day prior to the official announcement! The first few games had gone well and everyone was talking about the test match and the battle between Rob Howley and Joost van der Westhuizen. However, an innocuous tackle by the 20-stone giant Ollie le Roux in the Natal match led to a sharp pain in my shoulder and although I carried on for a short while it soon became apparent that my tour was at an end. Fortunately, I was selected for the tour to Australia in 2001 and played in two tests.

(v) Wasps's Heineken Cup triumph over Toulouse at Twickenham in 2004. The result was in the balance right into injury time – it was 20-20 when I decided to chance my arm with a short grubber kick within millimetres of the touchline. For some reason Poitrenaud, the Toulouse fullback, hesitated and in a moment of madness allowed me to touch down and seal the victory.

(vi) The magnificent four-year unbeaten run which we managed at Brynteg Comprehensive School during the 1980s.

Scott Gibbs's last-gasp try set up Neil Jenkins's match-winning conversion at Wembley, as Robert Howley's Wales made Wembley Welsh.

Jonathan Humphreys

Profile

For Cardiff, Bath and for his country, the fearsome and fearless hooker relished the physical aspects of the sport. He returned to skipper the national side in 2003 in the twilight of his career after Wales had suffered an embarrassing defeat against Italy at the Stadio Flaminio in Rome. They would be facing England, world champions in waiting. Wales lost the match but everyone agreed that Jonathan Humphreys had brought some pride and passion back into the Welsh performance. He's currently the forwards coach at the Ospreys, who are targeting the Heineken Cup in the near future after securing two Magners League titles and a recent EDF trophy win.

Jonathan Humphreys
on Filo Tiatia

Q Which was your first match as captain?

A **South Africa 40 Wales 11, September 2, 1995 (Ellis Park, Johannesburg). A real baptism of fire with Derwyn Jones carried off after only five minutes play having been punched by Kobus Wiese.**

Q Which were your best matches as captain?

A **(i) Wales 16 France 15, March 16, 1996 (Cardiff). A victory would have given Philippe Saint-Andre's XV the Five Nations Championship whilst we faced yet another whitewash. However, a stirring performance silenced the visitors.**
(ii) Wales 19 Australia 28, December 1, 1996 (Cardiff). We finally managed to challenge one of the world's best teams – in fact we led 19-18 with twenty minutes remaining. It was David

Campese's last international – 101 caps which included 64 tries.
(iii) Scotland 19 Wales 34, January 18, 1997 (Murrayfield).

Q Which was your finest hour as a rugby player?

A **(i) Winning my first cap for Wales against New Zealand at Ellis Park, Johannesburg in 1995.**
(ii) SWALEC Cup Final 1993 – Cardiff vs Llanelli. My grandfather was from Pontarddulais and a lifelong Scarlet supporter. I dare say he was a proud man that afternoon seeing his grandson in such ecstatic mood.

Q Who was the best captain you faced?

A **Will Carling**

Q Who was the best captain you played under?

A **Mike Hall**

Cardiff's Jonathan Humphreys
spots a rare gap between
Leicester's World Cup winners
Martin Johnson and Neil Back.

Billy
James
Profile

'Combative, in-your-face, explosive' just about sums up the former Aberavon, Swansea and Wales hooker Billy James, who led his country against Ireland at the National Stadium in April 1987, the very first player from Aberavon to captain the national side. In what was then an amateur game, the man from Taibach's attitude was truly professional, and he certainly made his presence felt on the field, relishing the physical aspects of the sport. However, Billy James was also a competent footballer, classy with ball in hand and constantly to be seen wrestling the ball away in tackle and maul situations, eagerly setting up attacking opportunities.

Ieuan Evans, try-scorer against Ireland in a losing cause, in Billy James's only match as captain.

Gethin Jenkins
Profile

Gethin Jenkins, the Cardiff Blues, Wales and British and Irish Lions loose-head prop forward, is the embodiment of the modern front-row forward. His talent straddles the contact areas of the scrum, ruck, maul, and line-out, but he also looks perfectly at home in the company of the speedsters and tricksters out wide. Always in the thick of the action, Gethin is also noted for his honesty and a determination to succeed. It was his powerful surge from loose play which caused Ronan O'Gara to panic in a Grand Slam decider in 2005. All in all, Gethin Jenkins is pure gold!

Adam Jones, Gethin Jenkins's partner-in-crime for Wales and the Lions, commandeers the Six Nations trophy in 2008.

77

Paul John
Profile

Pontypridd's famous halfback combination of Neil Jenkins and Paul John caused the fancied European teams to flounder during the late 1990s. Paul had a fast, accurate service, along with that innate knack of reading situations. The legendary Swansea and Wales scrum half, R.M. (Dickie) Owen, once wrote in an article in 1927, 'If you're going to pass do so at once, and from the very spot where you get the ball. If you decide to run, also do so at once, and keep thinking as you run.' Paul John, who recently guided Wales to their unbelievable World Sevens title, epitomised that very philosophy.

' The non-Welsh player I'd most like to have in my team. '

Paul John
on Bryan Habana

Alun Wyn Jones

Profile

The last four years have been significant ones for Alun Wyn Jones, of the Ospreys, Wales and the British and Irish Lions. Since winning his first cap as a wing forward against Argentina in Puerto Madryn in June 2006, he has gone on to establish himself as the first-choice second-row forward with region and country. However, Alun has also been busy studying law at Swansea University where he graduated in 2010. In the long term this is where his future may lie, but at the moment he is concentrating on his rugby and those in the know predict a glittering career as a player and captain.

❛ A schoolboy hero of mine. ❜

Alun Wyn Jones on John Eales

Duncan Jones

Profile

Always in the thick of the action, Duncan Jones, the former Neath and current Ospreys and Wales loose-head prop forward, has become almost a cult figure in Welsh rugby over the past decade. His long, blonde, curly and often dishevelled locks have made him instantly recognisable on the field of play, but he has all too often been sidelined during the last two seasons. Having been plagued by injury, the Blaengwynfi-born prop is however ready once again to return to the fray and bolster his regional team, as well as providing technique and muscle to Warren Gatland's Welsh front row.

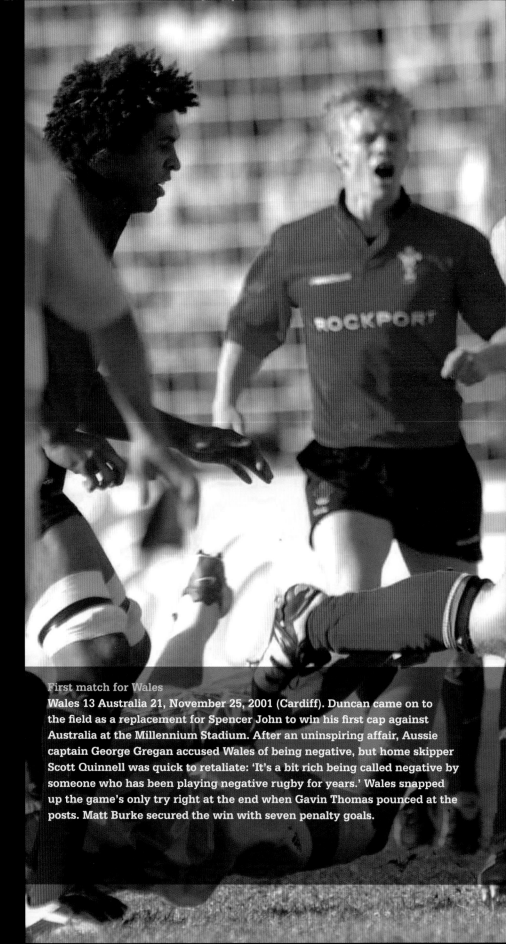

First match for Wales

Wales 13 Australia 21, November 25, 2001 (Cardiff). Duncan came on to the field as a replacement for Spencer John to win his first cap against Australia at the Millennium Stadium. After an uninspiring affair, Aussie captain George Gregan accused Wales of being negative, but home skipper Scott Quinnell was quick to retaliate: 'It's a bit rich being called negative by someone who has been playing negative rugby for years.' Wales snapped up the game's only try right at the end when Gavin Thomas pounced at the posts. Matt Burke secured the win with seven penalty goals.

The easily recognizable Duncan Jones on the charge against Argentina.

First match as captain

Argentina 27 Wales 25, June 11, 2006 (Raul Conti Stadium, Puerto Madryn, Patagonia). It was really bizarre. Supporters from both sides packed into the compact ground and spoke Welsh to each other! What's more the Patagonians present also sang *Hen Wlad fy Nhadau* with gusto!. It was Gareth Jenkins's first match in charge of the national side but his relatively inexperienced XV took the lead with tries from Mark Jones and Ian Evans. Juan Manuel Leguizamon and Jose Maria Nunez Piossek eventually responded for the home side. Ian Evans's try was a remarkable effort as the 21-year-old intercepted Agustin Pichot's pass in midfield and raced 45 metres to score under the posts. Leguizamon's try was hotly disputed as he seemed to have grounded the ball beyond the dead-ball line. Referee Alain Rolland inexplicably ignored Welsh claims to consult the video official. The highlight of an exciting match was Jamie Robinson's clinical break from deep inside his own 22-metre line which eventually saw James Hook, showing great strength, crossing underneath the posts. Final score – Argentina 27 Wales 25.

Gwyn Jones

Profile

Gwyn's glittering rugby career was tragically cut short by a horrific neck injury sustained during a Cardiff vs Swansea match at the Arms Park in 1997. But Gwyn's courage and determination ensured that all was not lost. Indeed a few years later Dr Gwyn Jones graduated from Cardiff University. What is more, he remained intent on making a contribution to Welsh rugby. A pundit on S4C and BBC Sport, Gwyn's astute and in-depth analysis have earned him great respect in Wales and beyond, as have his regular columns for the *Western Mail*. He is one of sport's great role models.

Gwyn Jones drags England's Paul Grayson with him, whilst John Davies drags Grayson back.

Q Which was your first match as captain?

A USA 20 Wales 30, July 5, 1997 (Wilmington, North Carolina). The team talk was held in a tent adjacent to the ground and it seemed at one stage that the match would be called off as a result of threatening weather conditions. And it was the occasion when Wales took the field with a midfield which must have totally confused the broadcasters present – Arwel Thomas, Leigh Davies and Gareth Thomas had all bleached their hair!

Q Which was your best match as captain?

A Wales 7 New Zealand 42, November 29, 1997 (Wembley). It was a great honour to lead Wales out at Wembley in front of 76,000 spectators. They were a powerful unit and although Sean Fitzpatrick was not fit enough to lead the side, he did appear as a replacement for the last 25 minutes winning his 92nd and final cap.

Q Which was your finest hour as a rugby player?

A Wales 16 France 15, March 19, 1996 (Cardiff) France were firm favourites: a win would have given them the championship and handed Wales the wooden spoon. In a great team performance, I was thrilled to have been named man-of-the-match.

Q Which current non-Welsh player would you love to have in your team?

A Richie McCaw (on the bench and on for the last twenty minutes after I've done all the hard work!)

Q Who was your most respected opponent?

A Laurent Cabannes

Q Who was the best captain you played under?

A Ieuan Evans

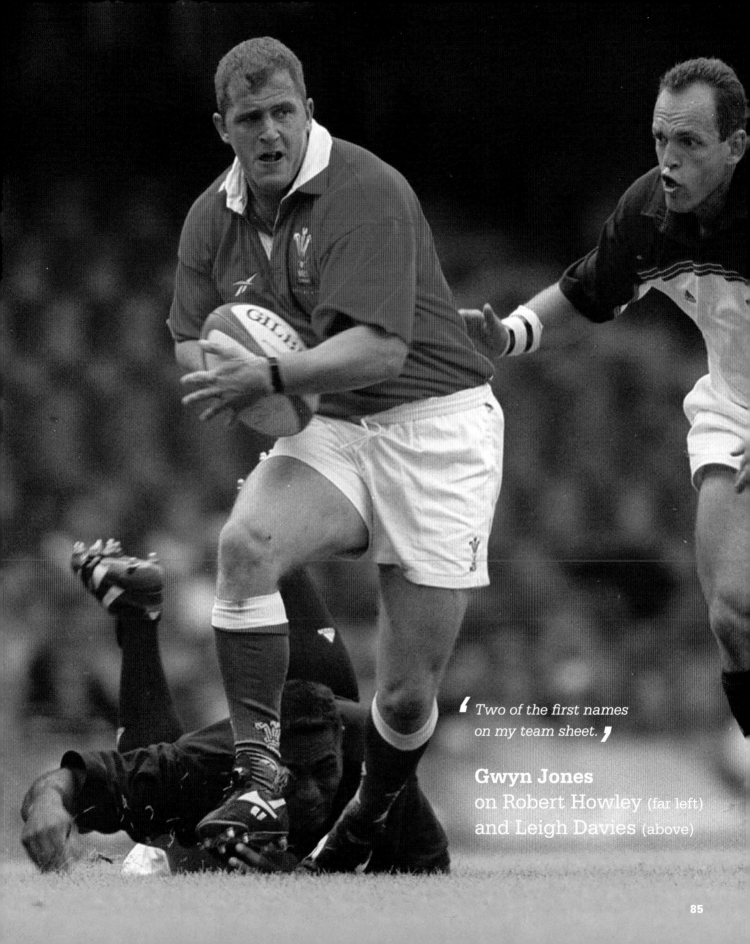

'Two of the first names on my team sheet.'

Gwyn Jones
on Robert Howley (far left)
and Leigh Davies (above)

I never faced a better No. 7.

Kingsley Jones
on Martyn Williams

Kingsley Jones

Profile

In the course of its rich history, Wales has managed to produce several world class open-side wing forwards. Ivor Jones was granted iconic status whilst touring New Zealand in 1930 and similar praise has been showered on Clem Thomas, Haydn Morgan, John Taylor and the magnificent Martyn Williams. They are the inspiration for the likes of Kingsley Jones, himself a workmanlike No.7 with a knack of intimidating the opposition and passing on scoring opportunities whenever they arose. After several successful seasons in Gloucester's back row, Kingsley is currently masterminding Sale's return to its former glory days.

Q Which was your finest hour as a rugby player?
A (i) South Africa 96 Wales 13, June 27, 1998
   (Loftus Versfeld, Pretoria). The agony and the
   ecstasy, or rather the ecstasy and the agony!
   It was the best and worst of times. I was
   asked to skipper the side when Robert Howley
   withdrew. Eighty minutes, fifteen tries and 96
   points later I have to admit the privilege had
   become somewhat of an embarrassment.
   (ii) Heineken Cup 2000/01. I'd ruptured my
   Achilles tendon prior to Rugby World Cup 1999
   but was appointed captain of Gloucester on
   my return. The Kingsholm faithful deserved
   success and it eventually came our way when
   we topped a tough group which included
   Colomiers and Llanelli. A great win over
   Cardiff took us into the semi final, where
   we narrowly lost to the eventual winners
   Leicester 19-15.

(iii) Leading Ebbw Vale to the final of the
SWALEC Cup at Bristol's Ashton Gate in 1998.

Q Who was your most respected opponent?
A Martyn Williams. I played with him in the
   back row when he represented Pontypridd for
   the first time against South Wales Police, and
   we both claimed our first caps in Wales's back
   row against the Barbarians in August 1996. He
   hasn't changed since those memorable Ponty
   days.

Q Who were your schoolboy rugby heroes?
A Terry Cobner and Bobby Windsor.

Q Who was the best captain you faced?
A Philippe Saint-Andre, my old pal, who
   somehow managed to captain the side
   successfully from the wing position.

Robert Jones

Profile

The scrum half from Trebannws scaled the heights of the game, and was an integral member of the triumphant British Lions side in Australia in 1989. As a result of application and ability, Robert managed to perfect all the skills in the scrum half's armoury. He was as two-footed a kicker as he was a two-handed passer, often to be seen dictating play subtly in defence and attack. He became the role model to scrum halves in both hemispheres mainly because his passing was always of the highest standard: there was no pronounced wind-up as he granted grateful three-quarters precious extra seconds.

Robert Jones
on Nick Farr-Jones

Q Which was your first match as captain?

A **Wales 9 New Zealand 34, November 4, 1989 (Cardiff). It was an awesome display by the All Blacks who proved throughout the afternoon that they could master the maul as well as the ruck. They were well led by the inspirational Wayne Shelford. We competed throughout and restricted the world champions to four tries. Gareth Llewellyn and Phil Pugh won their first caps.**

Q Which was your finest hour as a rugby player?

A **(i) Winning my first cap at Twickenham in January 1986.**
(ii) A series win for the British Lions in Australia in 1989.
(iii) A win against Australia to secure third place in the 1987 Rugby World Cup.

(iv) Swansea's magnificent win against the world champions, Australia, at St Helen's in 1992. We stuffed them!

Q Which current Welsh player would you love to have in your team?

A **Martyn Williams. One of the best footballers I've ever seen. He should have started for the Lions Test team on three tours.**

Q Who was the best captain you faced?

A **Will Carling**

Q Who were your most respected opponents?

A **Nick Farr-Jones and Gary Armstrong.**

Q Who was the best captain you played under?

A **Finlay Calder. He had great motivational qualities, was a real disciplinarian and a fine man.**

Along with Gerald Davies, he was my schoolboy hero.

Robert Jones
on Dave Loveridge

Ryan Jones

Profile

Who could ever hope to represent Wales, score a try in the red jersey, play for the British and Irish Lions in a Test match, score a try for the Lions in New Zealand, captain Wales and lead one's country during a Grand Slam season? It would be impossible to achieve all those things. Not if you're Ryan Jones. What's more, he's done it all in the space of five years and has managed to lead his regional side, the Ospreys, to two Magners League titles and an EDF trophy. The family's mantlepiece must stretch the length of the Gower Peninsula!

Ryan Jones celebrates the 2008 Grand Slam with (from l. to r.) Gethin Jenkins, Ian Gough and Jamie Roberts.

Q Which was your first match as captain?
A England 19 Wales 26, February 2, 2008 (Twickenham). What a day! It was our first win at Twickenham for 20 years and to be perfectly honest a victory seemed highly improbable as we trailed 16-6 at the interval. However, a grilling from new coach Warren Gatland resulted in an amazing second half comeback. The first try was psychologically important. James Hook danced around three tacklers and offloaded for Byrne to score. Moments later Mike Phillips charged down an Iain Balshaw clearance. Gethin Jenkins claimed the loose ball, which led to the influential Phillips diving in at the corner. As you can imagine we were all in ecstatic mood – if this was captaincy, then I wanted more!

Q Which was your finest hour as a rugby player?
A (i) Wales 36 South Africa 38 November 6, 2004 (Cardiff). My first cap!

(ii) Scotland 22 Wales 46, March 13, 2005 (Murrayfield). My first international try in a record win, during that never-to-be-forgotten Grand Slam season.
(iii) Being called out to join the British Lions in 2005, before playing in all three Tests.
(iv) Being part of that stand-off against the Haka has to be a pretty special moment!
(v) Captaining Wales to a Grand Slam in 2008.
(vi) Two Magners League titles and an EDF Trophy win for the Ospreys.

Q Who were your schoolboy heroes?
A Steffan Edberg, Ryan Giggs, Peter Schmeichel and Eric Cantona.

Q Who are your most respected opponents?
A It has to be the next one! I've come across some pretty tough back-row row forwards over the years, but New Zealand's Jerry Collins, Richie McCaw and South Africa's Schalk Burger are probably the toughest.

RYAN JONES Q&A

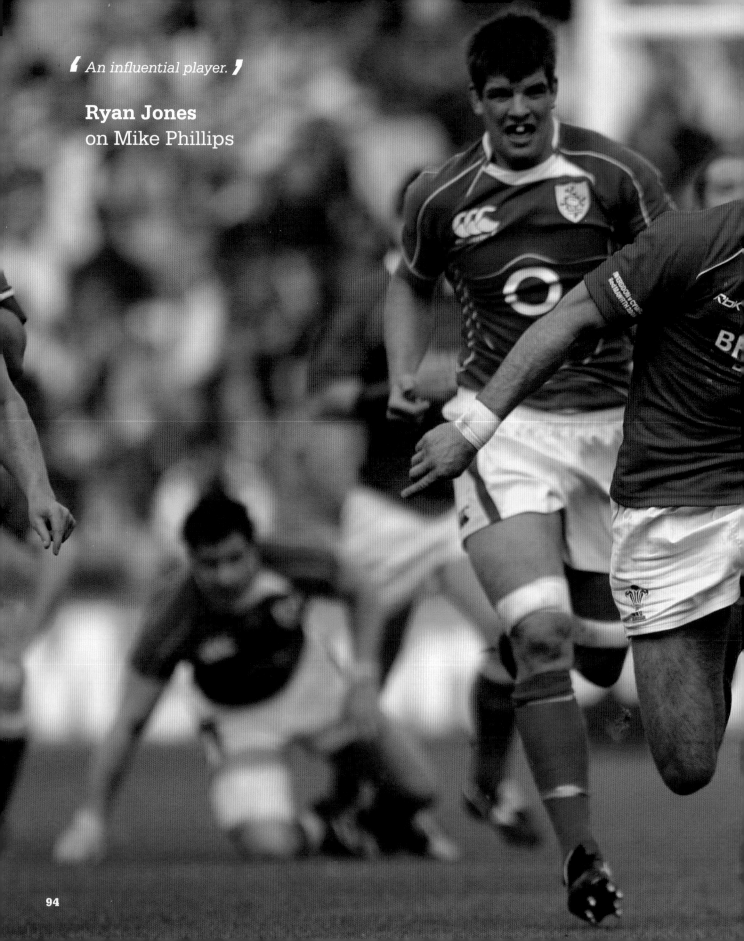

'*An influential player.*'

Ryan Jones
on Mike Phillips

Stephen Jones

Profile

Stephen Jones's contribution to Llanelli, Clermont Auvergne, the Scarlets, Wales and the British Lions has been immense – imposing in defence, creative in attack and with an all-round kicking game that has allowed him to accumulate points from all angles. In Roger Anderson's *Mr Men* series, he is Mr Dependable! Stephen has been pivotal in Wales's recent Grand Slam successes and if there is one game that typifies his all-round talents, it is that match played against France at the Stade de France in 2005 – his surging run from his own 22 was the defining moment in Wales's spectacular victory. In years to come we will all come to appreciate Stephen Jones's greatness as a rugby player.

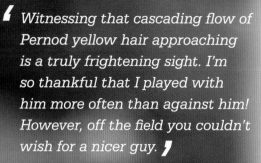

Witnessing that cascading flow of Pernod yellow hair approaching is a truly frightening sight. I'm so thankful that I played with him more often than against him! However, off the field you couldn't wish for a nicer guy.

Stephen Jones
on Aurelien Rougerie

Q Which was your best match as captain?
A **Wales 72 Japan 18, September 20, 2007 (Cardiff). It was the Rugby World Cup match when Shane Williams, winning his 50th cap for his country, passed Ieuan Evans's try-scoring record for Wales. It was an emphatic victory and put us in good heart prior to our final pool match against Fiji in Nantes. Japan contributed to an exciting encounter scoring two fine tries which included a quite spectacular length-of-the-field effort finished off with some aplomb by wing three-quarter Kosuta Endo. It was to prove one of the tries of the tournament.**

Q Which was your finest hour as a rugby player?
A **Wales 32 Ireland 20, March 19, 2005 (Cardiff). I could reminisce for hours on end and list many** memorable occasions. **The definitive moment could have been on the 2009 British Lions tour to South Africa when we should have clinched a series win. However, the hour or so at the end of the Grand Slam match against Ireland in 2005 was an important and significant period in my career as an international fly half. There had been many disappointments and suddenly we proved to our supporters, our critics and to ourselves that we were talented individuals.**

Q Who is the best captain you faced?
A **Martin Johnson**

Q Who is your most respected opponent?
A **Dan Carter**

Q Who is the best captain you've played under?
A **Robin McBryde at Llanelli RFC.**

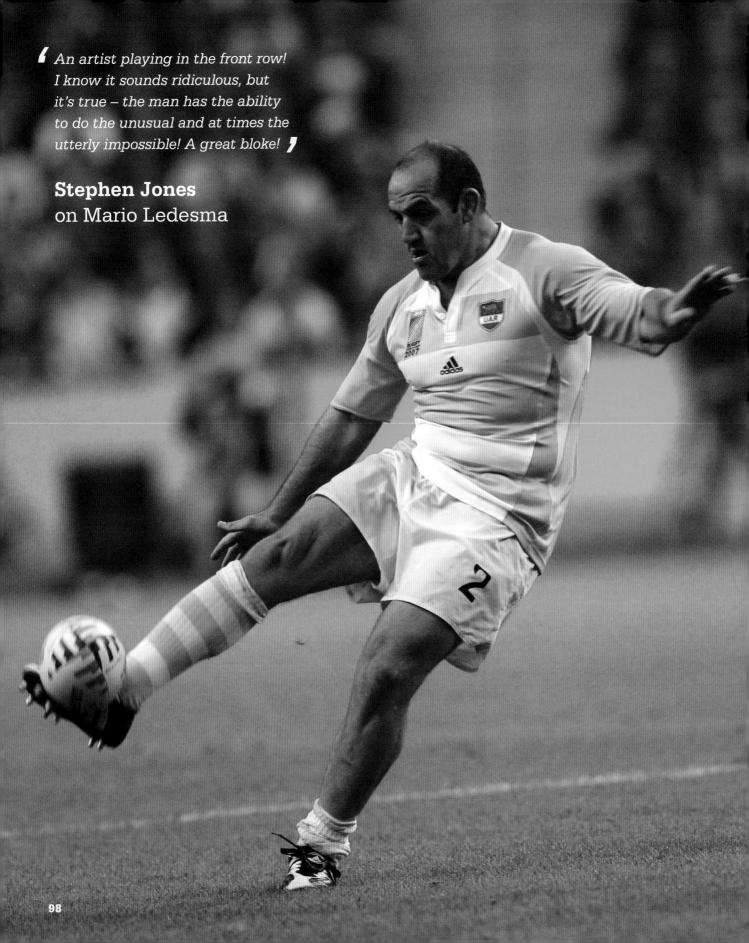

'An artist playing in the front row!
I know it sounds ridiculous, but
it's true – the man has the ability
to do the unusual and at times the
utterly impossible! A great bloke!'

Stephen Jones
on Mario Ledesma

Neil Jenkins, one of Stephen Jones's predecessors in the Welsh No. 10 shirt, and one who has helped Stephen become one of the world's premier kickers.

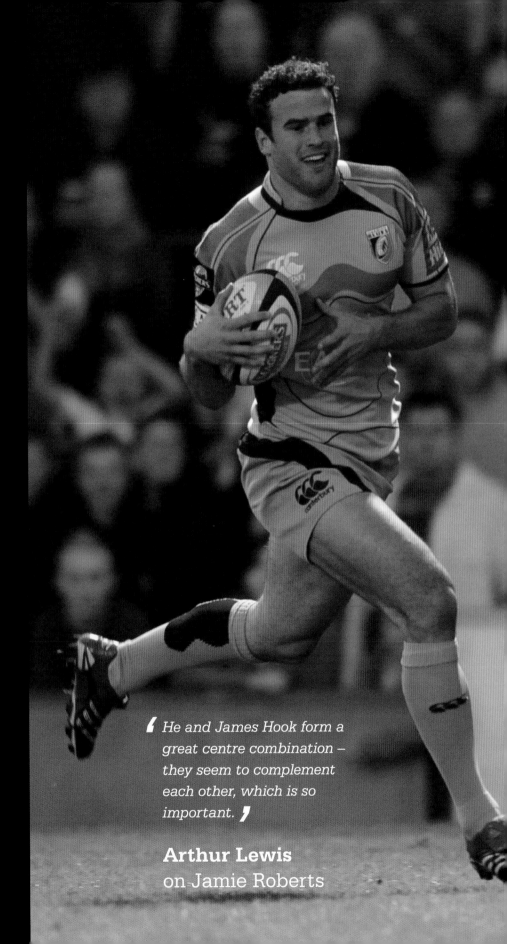

Arthur Lewis

Profile

Arthur Lewis of Ebbw Vale, Wales and the British Lions is a North Monmouthshire legend. He was labelled a crash-ball centre three-quarter as much for his robust physique as his manner of play, and it is true to say, however, that he would have struck fear into the heart of anyone who might have met him in a dark alley in Cordell's industrial landscape. But he could also be creative when necessary and several attacking moves implemented at Ebbw Vale were often used by Wales at international level with Arthur himself playing a pivotal role in each one.

He and James Hook form a great centre combination – they seem to complement each other, which is so important.

Arthur Lewis
on Jamie Roberts

Gareth Llewellyn

Profile

Tall, athletically built, totally committed – Gareth Llewellyn seemed to have been designed by computer for the role of second-row forward. He took the rugby world by storm in the late 1980s when he burst on to the scene as a nineteen-year-old for Neath against New Zealand at the Gnoll. His ability to win the ball at the line-out was uncanny, whether it was with his clean catching of the ball or by his deft tap-downs to his scrum half. He won 90 caps for Wales during a fifteen-year period and whilst others threatened to displace him, Gareth proved himself the consummate professional.

❛ I'd want him in my team. ❜

Gareth Llewellyn
on Ma'a Nonu

John Lloyd
Profile

Wales has produced so many strong and mobile prop forwards who also looked comfortable with the ball in hand. Think of Barry Llewelyn (the Martin Peters of the rugby world, who seemed to be three decades ahead of his time), Denzil Williams, Graham Price, Glyn Shaw, David Young, Gethin Jenkins, Adam Jones and John Lloyd, who became the first Welsh prop to captain the national team. John was a fine seven-a-side exponent, looking more of an outside half than a scrum worker. With his beloved Bridgend, or in his capacity as Welsh National Coach, John was a true professional in those far-away amateur days. He was a whisker away from joining the select band of Welsh Grand Slam captains, but, after three straight victories in 1972, Wales declined to visit Dublin as a result of a terrorist threat.

The best wing three-quarter playing in world rugby at the moment. He can turn a game in the twinkling of an eye.

John Lloyd
on Shane Williams

Jack
Matthews
Profile

Dynamic in defence;
blistering in attack. That
about sums up the skills
of Dr Jack Matthews who
terrorised defences in the
1940s and early 1950s.
According to Dai Smith
and Gareth Williams in
Fields of Praise, Matthews
was a human cannon-ball,
constantly applying full
frontal shock-treatment with
his shoulders, and acquiring
Claude Davey's reputation
of being the most aggressive
tackler in Welsh rugby. 'Once
Jackie Matthews committed
himself to the tackle,' wrote
Fred Allen, 'the next person
to arrive on the scene should
have been the rag-and-bone
collector.' His partnership
with Bleddyn Williams for
Cardiff, Wales and the British
Lions is legendary.

Bleddyn Williams, Jack
Matthews's illustrious
centre partner

Bryn Meredith

Profile

Bryn Victor Meredith was acclaimed in 1955 as one of the greatest players in his position to have visited South Africa. He was, along with W.O. (Billy) Williams and Courtney Meredith, a member of an all-Welsh front row. In 14 appearances as hooker on tour, he scored six tries which certainly impressed the hard-to-please South Africans. Bryn was tough as teak and exploded into the tackle area with fearless determination and spirit. However, he also had good hands, speed off the mark, and an ability to swerve and change pace dramatically. In today's professional world Bryn Meredith would have been worth his weight in gold.

He would be my outside half in a Dream Welsh XV.

Bryn Meredith on Cliff Morgan

Andy Moore

Profile

Without possession from scrum, line-out, ruck or maul, the most gifted wing three-quarters on the planet are surplus to requirement. Andy Moore, the only North Walian to have captained Wales, was a talented line-out jumper who served Swansea and Wales consistently before injuries forced him into retirement at the age of twenty-eight. Andy was blessed with silky hands which came from his decision to play basketball at an early age. He captained Wales on just the two occasions out in Osaka and Tokyo in 2001, with the management blooding several players who went on to serve their country with distinction.

He would have been an asset in any Welsh team.

Andy Moore
on Gethin Jenkins

Cliff Morgan
Profile

Many knowledgeable rugby critics still believe that the former pupil of Tonyrefail Grammar School, nurtured and developed by sports master Ned Gribble, is the finest in a long line of Welsh fly halves. Cliff Morgan's exploits on the 1955 British Lions tour of South Africa are the stuff of legends. The First Test in front of a record 96,000 crowd at Ellis Park, Johannesburg was on a knife edge. Reg Sweet takes up the story: 'From a scrummage Jeeps fed Morgan and in an instant the outside half had come and gone . . . It was all pace and co-ordination and perfection of judgement, as fine a try as you could wish to see.' The Lions won the match 23-22 and drew the series 2-2. Cliff Morgan remains a perceptive and articulate observer of the game, and is one of Wales's favourite sons.

He excites me. He is always anxious for the ball; is brave enough to take chances; is a brilliant sidestepping runner; is startlingly fast and a great try-scorer.

Cliff Morgan
on Shane Williams

Q Which was your best match as captain?
A **England 3 Wales 8, January 21, 1956 (Twickenham). My first game as captain.**

Q Which was your worst match as captain?
A **Ireland 11 Wales 3, March 10, 1956 (Lansdowne Road). We were all set to win the Triple Crown but Ireland, inspired by the great Jack Kyle, were too good for us.**

Q Which was your finest hour as a rugby player?
A **Either Wales beating the All Blacks at Cardiff in 1953 by 13 points to 8, or the First Lions Test against South Africa in Johannesburg in 1955 in front of a crowd of some 100,000, including the great Nelson Mandela, who was there, as he later told Tony O'Reilly of Ireland, before his incarceration on Robben Island, 'to shout for the Lions!' The Lions eventually triumphed by 23 points to 22. It is a game still talked about, fifty-five years later, as the greatest Test match ever played in South Africa.**

Q Which current Wales player would you love to have in your team?
A **Shane Williams**

Q Which current non-Welsh player would you love to have in your team?
A **Brian O'Driscoll**

Q Who was the best captain you faced?
A **Hennie Muller (South Africa 1951/52) was a remarkable No.8 forward; a great tackler with an outstanding rugby brain. He was greased lightning about the field and a true leader of men.**

Q Who would captain your Dream Welsh XV?
A **Bleddyn Williams, the dazzling try-making and try-scoring centre, who was tactically brilliant and had a genuine love of the game. He was a born leader and an inspiration to the team.**

Cliff Morgan's Dream Welsh XV

15   LEWIS JONES (Llanelli)
What talent! He was the first of a new breed of fullbacks for he was never concerned about safety first but was always seeking opportunity and adventure. He was a thrilling all-round player who had all the gifts of a midfield player. He was selected for the Lions at 19 years of age in 1950 in New Zealand. To make his armoury complete he was also a prodigious goal-kicker. A star of Rugby Union and Rugby League.

14   GERALD DAVIES (Cardiff, London Welsh and Cambridge University)
A natural, sidestepping player who was poetry in motion. A wonderful try-scorer. I saw him score four tries for the Lions in New Zealand against Hawke's Bay – each of them very different displaying his broad range of talents. One try was all about pace and timing, another was a chip ahead in his own 25, before gathering and sprinting 50 yards, the third was a glorious outside break whilst the fourth was a thrilling series of sidesteps and blistering speed to shatter the defence. I sat and watched in awe and wonder.

13   BLEDDYN WILLIAMS (Cardiff)
The Prince of Centres in my opinion. He could sidestep off either foot; was a most beautiful passer of the ball; a sound defender; a fine tackler and he read the game perfectly. Bleddyn was very tactically aware and a fine captain. He made other members of his team look good. New Zealand loved his style on the Lions Tour of 1950.

12   RAY GRAVELL (Llanelli)
The most passionate Welshman I have ever known. He was tough and strong and talented and he displayed this in majestic form for Llanelli, Wales and the Lions. He was a man's man and was loved and respected by both teammates and opponents alike. The personal motto of Sir Tasker Watkins VC, former President of the Welsh Rugby Union was '*Gwna dy ddyletswydd heb ystyried hunan-les*'. 'Do your duty without self-interest.' That was the defining spirit of Ray Gravell.

11   KEN JONES (Newport)
An Olympic sprinter who thrilled the rugby world in the 1950s. He scored so many superb tries for his club, Wales and the Lions. He too had a wonderful tour of New Zealand in 1950 playing outside Jack Kyle, Bleddyn Wiliams and Jack Matthews. He was adored by New Zealand fans for not only was he fast and elusive but also a devastating tackler.

10   BARRY JOHN (Llanelli and Cardiff)
The very mention of his name prompts the ecstasy of a religious revival! He invented Utopia! Like all world-class sportsmen he always seemed to have time to do anything he wanted to control the game. Barry was, for me, the classic outside half, beautifully balanced, carrying the ball in both hands, and a perceptive reader of the game. He was also a prodigious goal-kicker. Barry had supreme confidence. New Zealand called him King John. Absolutely right.

9   GARETH EDWARDS (Cardiff)
I consider Gareth to be the finest all-round rugby player the world has ever seen. Even in school he was supreme in gymnastics and athletics, excelling in the long jump, the hurdles and the pole vault. He could have been an Olympian if rugby had not captured his imagination. Gareth graced the game with great style and had the knack of scoring crucial tries just before or straight after the interval – 20 unforgettable tries in 53 consecutive internationals.

1   GRAHAM PRICE (Pontypool)
Like Gareth, Graham could have been an international athlete – in discus and shot. Happily he opted for a distinguished career in the front row of the scrum for Wales and on three Lions tours and in 552 games for his club. Majestic in the rough and tumble of the front row, he was amazingly fast and elusive in the loose. He played more Test Matches for the Lions than any other prop forward – the Prince of Props.

2   BRYN MEREDITH (Newport)
I played in the Welsh Secondary Schools International side with Bryn in 1949! He was great then and I followed his climb to fame into the Welsh XV and in 1955 shared his joy of the Lions tour in South Africa. In fact he made two further Lions tours, to New Zealand in 1959 and again to South Africa in 1962. There is no question about it, he was exceptional as a hooker. He was a fabulous forward in set scrums and in broken play – a natural for any Hall of Fame.

3   COURTNEY MEREDITH (Neath)
For some reason I have a soft spot for prop forwards for they inevitably exude that delicious difference which comes from being cheek by jowl with the opposition in the darkness of rhe scrum. Courtney is one of these and is regarded as one of the finest props ever to play for Wales and the Lions. In this age of specialisation we may not see his like again.

4   R.H. WILLIAMS (Llanelli)
Apart from all his heroic games for Llanelli and Wales, I think the match that put RH up with the greatest was the Lions' final Test against New Zealand in Eden Park, Auckland in 1959. Despite the unusually wet day, the Lions decided to run the ball. There were brilliant tries from Peter Jackson and Bev Risman but could the Lions hold out until the end for a win? Yes, for RH won every one of the last five line-outs – both the New Zealand's throw-ins and his own team's throw-ins!

5   ROY JOHN (Neath)
He must be one of the finest line-out jumpers ever. Years before lifting was allowed, Roy could spring to great heights to win the ball. What an athlete – what perfect timing. A must for Wales and Lions team of my era.

6   DAI MORRIS (Neath)
For a man who stood over six feet tall and weighed a mere 12 stone, he made every inch and ounce count. He was all sinew and bone. He was known as 'Dai the Shadow' – for he was never more than ten yards from the ball. He tackled furiously and supported brilliantly. My sort of flank forward.

8   MERVYN DAVIES (London Welsh and Swansea)
It was only six weeks after his first game for London Welsh that Mervyn played for Wales. He became a Lion in New Zealand in 1971 and he proved in his play that he should rate alongside Brian Lochore of New Zealand, Hennie Muller of South Africa and Des O'Brien of Ireland as one of the all-time greats in the No. 8 position.

7   R.C.C. THOMAS (Swansea and Cambridge University)
I select Clem for he was so highly respected and feared by the opposition. He was a strong tackler who terrified opposing halfbacks but what set him apart was his instinctive sense for positional play and his ability to read the game. Outstanding in broken play and more than useful when forward play was rough and tough. Top man.

Cliff Morgan carries five great Welsh fly halves on his shoulders. (From l. to r.) Groggs of himself, Dai Watkins, Barry John, Phil Bennett and Jonathan Davies.

Richard Moriarty
Profile

Richard Moriarty of Swansea
and Wales was a free spirit.
He rejected convention;
conforming was anathema
to him. On the rugby field
he was a giant – he had
the strength and power
to hold his own in most
situations. However, it
was in the line-out that
he came into his own. He
consistently won his own
ball, soaring into the air with
consummate ease, ensuring
clean possession, either by
catching the ball cleanly or
palming accurately to his
scrum half. He was also a
master in defensive lines-
out, constantly harassing
the opposition and generally
making their life a misery.
He led Wales to their best-
ever World Cup finish, third
behind New Zealand and
France in 1987.

' My sort of player. '

Richard Moriarty
on Ian Gough

Robert Norster

Profile

Robert Norster was a highly-acclaimed technician who ruled the line-out throughout Europe in the 1980s. He was born and bred in Blaenau Gwent and briefly plied his trade for Abertillery before joining Cardiff, and excelling for the capital city's team. He went on to represent Wales on 34 occasions and the British Lions on their tours to New Zealand in 1983 and Australia in 1989. It's true to say that Robert Norster, who is well-liked and respected in rugby circles throughout the world, is one of Wales's finest second-row forwards.

If we can look beyond the infamous diving incident, Andy Haden was a very special if often controversial figure throughout his long and distinguished career.

Robert Norster on Andy Haden

Michael Owen

Profile

To some, Michael Owen represents the cool and calculating goalscorer who tormented defences whilst representing Liverpool, Newcastle, Manchester United and England. To others, images abound of an unorthodox, and possibly ungainly, No. 8 forward blessed with golden hands, delivering what Jonathan Davies would describe as 'the money ball'.

Indeed, Michael Owen of Pontypridd, the Celtic Warrriors, Newport Gwent Dragons, Saracens, Wales and the British and Irish Lions would have thrilled basketball icons such as Michael Jordan and Scotty Pippen. He will also be remembered fondly for his all-round play and leadership skills during the 2005 Grand Slam campaign.

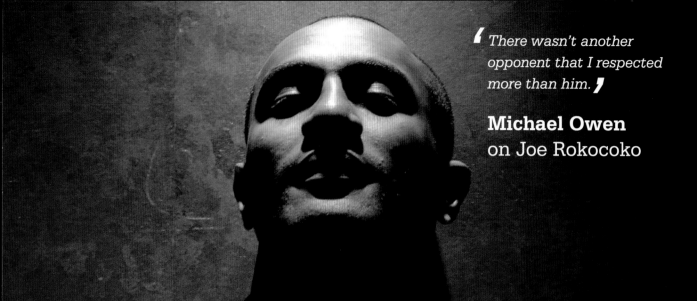

Q Which was your first match as captain?
A **France 18 Wales 24, February 26, 2005 (Stade de France). It won't count in the record books but will forever register in the Owen household as the day I captained Wales during the second half of a sensational rugby match. Officially, my first match as captain was the convincing victory against Scotland at Murrayfield three weeks later when we defeated Gordon Bulloch's men 46-22.**

Q Which was your best match as captain?
A **Wales 32 Ireland 20, March 19, 2005 (Cardiff). The Millennium Stadium was packed to capacity, the city centre a mass of red and green with the area in and around City Hall suitably dressed with big screens to accommodate 15,000 ticketless fans. It was our first Grand Slam in 27 years and a time to celebrate the present rather than re-live past memories. The thunderous roar at Chris White's final whistle could be heard throughout the land.**

Q Which current non-Welsh player would you love to have in your team?
A **Dan Carter**

Q Who was the best captain you faced?
A **Brian O'Driscoll**

Q Who was the best captain you played under?
A **Gareth Thomas**

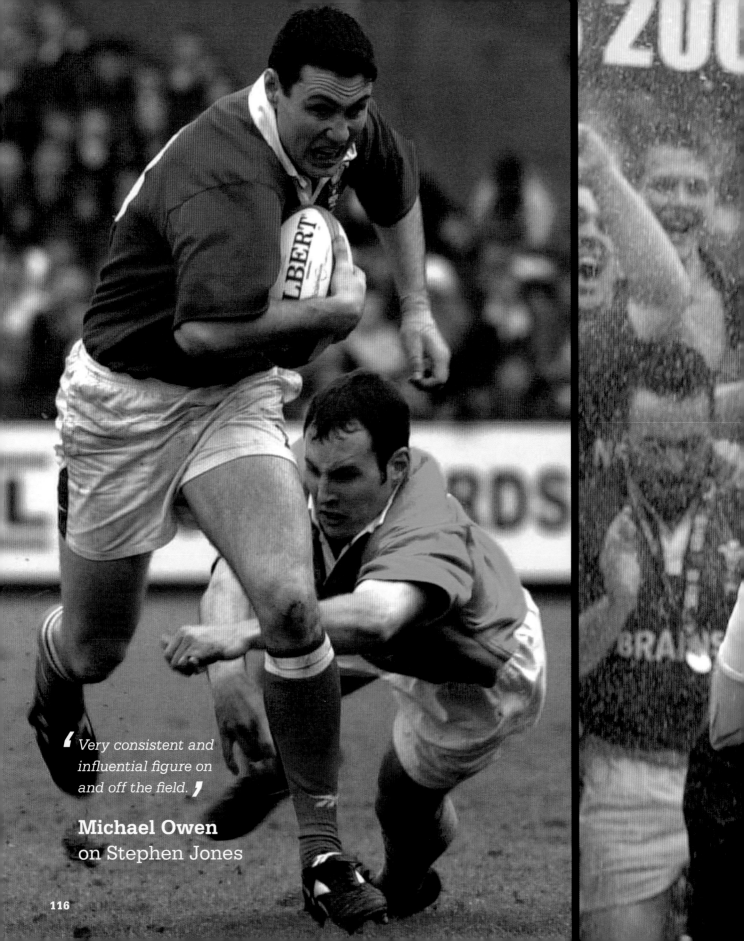

Very consistent and influential figure on and off the field.

Michael Owen
on Stephen Jones

Injured captain Gareth Thomas and playing captain Michael Owen lead their team's Grand Slam celebrations in 2005.

Dwayne Peel

Profile

Dwayne possesses all the attributes of a modern-day scrum half. He also has that extra dimension which enables him to vary attacks, and is often to be seen running menacingly from short penalties where his pace, penetration, precision and persistence can prove lethal. He is a creative force not to be underestimated, and woe betide the complacent defence who fail to police him from kick-off to final whistle. He has made telling contributions at club level for Llanelli Scarlets and Sale Sharks, and at international level for Wales – with whom he won the Grand Slam in 2005 – and the British Lions.

The best scrum half I've played against.

Dwayne Peel on Byron Kelleher

Kevin Phillips
Profile

Kevin Phillips will always be associated with Neath Rugby Football Club and a front row which traumatised and terrorised opponents during the late 1980s and early 1990s. The late (and great) Brian Williams, Kevin Phillips and John Davies were three dairy farmers from deepest West Wales whose smiles were warm and mischievous during weekly marts. However, that all changed on Saturday afternoons. In three consecutive seasons between 1988 and 1991 the Welsh All Blacks swept all before them, and it was no surprise that the tour to Namibia included nine players from the champion club, with Kevin Phillips captaining the squad.

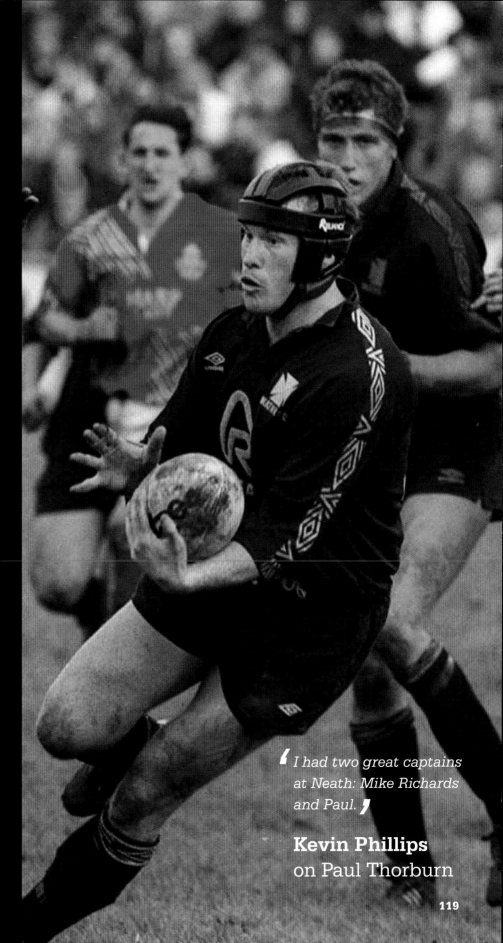

❛I had two great captains at Neath: Mike Richards and Paul.❜

Kevin Phillips
on Paul Thorburn

David Pickering

Profile

Committed and constantly at hand to intimidate the opposition, but also a creative runner *par excellence*, who seemed to be ever present in passing on scoring opportunities when they came, David Pickering was an outstanding openside wing forward. In 1986, David led a squad to the South Sea Islands and three Tests in Fiji, Tonga and Western Samoa – a destination which could be described as idyllic. However, a kick on his head against Fiji saw him return home prematurely. His love for the game never diminished and retirement saw him serving his country and the world of rugby with distinction as a manager, administrator and International Board Member.

> *A superb leader who just inspired his men on and off the field.*

David Pickering
on Derek Quinnell

Q Which was your first match as captain?

A **England 21 Wales 18, January 18, 1986 (Twickenham). It was the Rob Andrew Show! We scored the only try of the match but lost as a result of Rob Andrew's expertise – he kicked six penalties with his right foot and just to highlight his versatility he slotted a dropped goal with his left foot.**

Q Which was your finest hour as a rugby palyer?

A **(i) Scoring two tries for Wales at Murrayfield in 1985.**
(ii) Wales 13 England 13, February 5, 1983 (Cardiff). What a day! It was a tense affair with first caps for Malcolm Dacey, Mark Ring, Mark Wyatt, Billy James and myself. England arrived at Cardiff having lost the previous nine matches at the Arms Park. Jeff Squire
and John Carleton scored the tries and it ended all square at 13-13.
(iii) Schweppes Cup Finals were memorable occasions and I was fortunate to have played in four – two for Llanelli and two for Neath.

Q Who were your schoolboy rugby heroes?

A **Gareth Edwards, Dai Morris (what a player), and the great Neath sides of the early 1970s. They won the Cup Final in 1972 and I was there to support my heroes. Outside half Dai Parker orchestrated play and ensured an All Blacks victory.**

Q Who was the best captain you played under?

A **The warrior Derek Quinnell.**

Q Who were your most respected opponents?

A **Peter Winterbottom and Graham Mourie.**

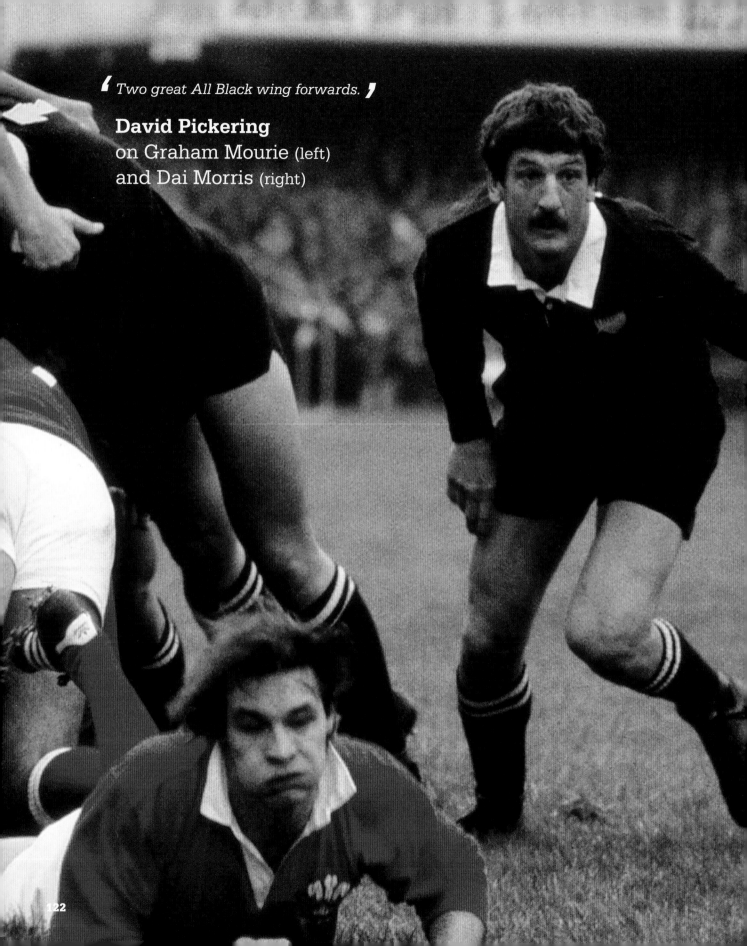

' Two great All Black wing forwards. '

David Pickering
on Graham Mourie (left)
and Dai Morris (right)

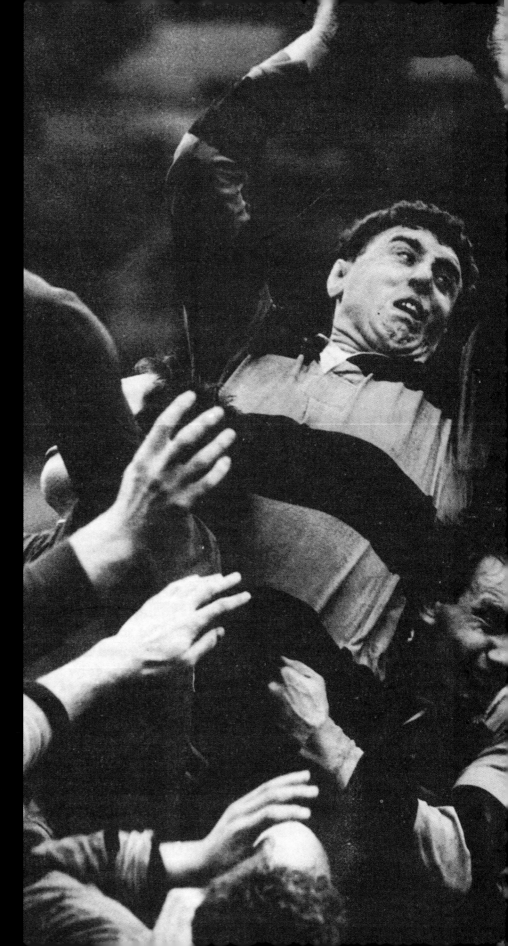

Brian Price

Profile

A superb line-out forward with a genuine physical presence, Brian Price was one of the finest second-row forwards of his generation. He, like so many other Newport forwards of the late 1950s and 1960s, were outstanding seven-a-side players who could also have excelled on the basketball courts. Brian has always been an excellent ambassador for the game. Off the field he was a gentleman, but once he donned the black-and-amber Newport jersey or the red jersey of Wales or the British Lions, he caused chaos in opposition ranks. Sometimes creative, sometimes destructive, Brian Price proved himself to be a truly great rugby player.

Although I played with fabulous No. 7s in Dai Hayward, Haydn Morgan, Alan Thomas and John Taylor, it would have been great to see what Martyn could do playing in a decent pack of forwards.

Brian Price
on Martyn Williams

Q Which was your best match as captain?
A **France 8 Wales 8, March 22, 1969 (Stade Colombes). The only match Wales did not lose in Paris during the 1960s. If we had won it we would have claimed the Grand Slam for the first time since 1952. Phil Bennett became Wales's first ever replacement when Gerald Davies left the field injured. (Ian McRae, the Scottish scrum half, was the first Five Nations substitute, whilst Mike Gibson became the very first international replacement — for the Lions in South Africa in 1968.)**

Q Which was your worst match as captain?
A **Wales 24 Ireland 11, March 8, 1969 (Cardiff). A really violent game! I lost my cool, lashed out at Noel Murphy and should perhaps have been sent off by referee D.C.J. McMahon from Scotland.**

Q Who was the first name on your team sheet?
A **Gareth Edwards**

Q Which current non-Welsh player would you love to have in your team?
A **Imanol Harinordoquy. He's a Basque so he should be able to sing! A terrific player using sublime basketball skills, he might be the answer to our poor line-out.**

Q Who was the best captain you faced?
A **Walter Spanghero**

BRIAN PRICE Q&A

Scott Quinnell

Profile

Scott Quinnell, as befits the family tradition, was a cult hero at Stradey Park where his riproaring appearances in the Scarlet jersey were a source of delight to the vociferous supporters who revelled in his charging, high-octane runs. There was no finer sight on a rugby field than to see Scott Quinnell breaking from a scrum, decimating the opposing defence, twisting and turning and more often than not ploughing over the try line. 'Great Scott!' An apt epithet for one who succeeded in straining nerve and sinew for a worthy cause for Llanelli, Richmond, Wigan, Wales and the British Lions.

*He would make the tackles
I never made!*

Scott Quinnell
on Richie McCaw

Q Which was your first match as captain?

A **Wales 13 South Africa 23, November 2000
(Cardiff). With ten minutes to go it was 13-
13 and when Robbie Fleck was sin-binned I
was confident we could gain a second victory
against the mighty Springboks. It was not to be
as Braam van Straaten stroked a penalty and
Breyton Paulse raced away for the crucial score.**

Q Which was your finest hour as a rugby player?

A **(i) My try against France at Cardiff in 1994 in
our first success against them in 12 seasons.
I stole away from a line-out and managed to
escape the clutches of several Frenchmen, just
steered clear of the touchline and crossed in the
corner.
(ii) Australia 13 British Lions 29, June 2001
(Brisbane). Playing for the British Lions was an
opportunity to emulate my father Derek and my
uncle, Barry John.
(iii) Llanelli 25 Wasps 15, December 2001
(Stradey Park). We had to win by 10 points in**

**order to qualify for the Quarter Final stages of
the Heineken, Cup and we didn't just win – we
destroyed them! It was an important match; it
was live on BBC Grandstand with the great Bill
McLaren making his first and only visit to the
historical venue.**

Q Which opposing captain made the most
impression?

A **Martin Johnson. I was also fortunate enough
to have played with him on numerous
occasions. I'd run through a brick wall for the
man – mind you, he would have shattered the
brickwork prior to my arrival!**

Q Who were your most respected opponents?

A **There were so many, including Wayne 'Buck'
Shelford – I once scored a try against him for
Llanelli at Northampton and managed a wry
smile in his direction as I made my way back
to the halfway line. Thankfully I don't think he
saw it!**

Clive Rowlands

Profile

Captain, coach, competitor, chairman, commentator, chorister. And if you also add charisma, character and charm to the mixture . . hey presto! it's Clive from Cwmtwrch! D.C.T. Rowlands's contribution to rugby and to life in Wales has been immense; his inspirational leadership as scrum half and captain led to a Triple Crown for Wales during the 1964/65 season, whilst he also played a significant managerial role in the three Grand Slam successes of the 1970s. As manager of the successful British Lions tour to Australia in 1989, he was one of rugby's finest ambassadors. Clive Rowlands really has done it

'The player I most enjoyed captaining.'

Clive Rowlands
on David Watkins

Q Which was your best match as captain?
A **Wales 14 Ireland 8, March 13, 1965 (Cardiff). It was a Triple Crown decider. After a fiery first few minutes, Ray McLoughlin and I were told by referee Peter Brookes (RFU) to control our respective teams, or the next culprit would be dismissed! My forwards asked me what the referee had said. I replied, 'He just told me the dinner's at the Angel Hotel and you're all playing well!'**

Q Who was the first name on your team sheet?
A **When I was captain, it would be Brian Thomas; when I was coach, Gareth Edwards.**

Q Which current Welsh player would you love to have in your team?
A **Shane Williams**

Q Which current non-Welsh player would you love to have in your team?
A **Victor Matfield (South Africa). Line-out possession is vital and Matfield seems to dominate this phase of play. A true Trojan in all other aspects of the game.**

Q Who was the best captain you faced?
A **Wilson Whineray (New Zealand). I played against him for Wales in 1963 when we lost 6-0.**

A coach's dream.

Clive Rowlands
on Gareth Edwards

Jeff Squire

Profile

Jeff Squire was a great back-row forward and in another team in another era would have been classed amongst the greats. For Newport, Pontypool, Wales and the British Lions, he was revered for his physical and mental strength, his commitment, endurance and resilience, but he was also a very creative back-row forward with ball in hand, whether he was at No. 8 or blind-side wing forward. The first of his 29 caps came against Ireland at Cardiff in January 1977 – a match remembered for the first sending off in the history of the International Championship when referee Norman Sanson dismissed Geoff Wheel and Willie Duggan.

A rampant Jeff Squire, with fellow Pontypool wing forward Terry Cobner in support, makes ground for the 1977 British Lions in New Zealand

First and second matches as captain

(i) Wales 18 France 9, January 19, 1980 (Cardiff). It was a historic day in the history of Welsh rugby football – the two-tier East Terrace was opened for over 13,000 supporters with a tailor-made enclosure for approximately 1,500 schoolchildren. The electronic scoreboard was also used for the first time and for the statisticians in our midst it was the first time Wales had managed four tries against France in Cardiff for 30 years with Elgan Rees, Terry Holmes, David Richards and Graham Price crossing.

(ii) England 9 Wales 8, February 16, 1980 (Twickenham). We lost by a whisker. Wales played virtually throughout with fourteen men after referee David Burnett sent Paul Ringer from the field of play for a fairly innocuous tackle on England's John Horton. Paul had possibly been fortunate to last the 80 minutes against France at Cardiff. Indeed a number of television programmes including *Newsnight* drew detailed attention to some of his transgressions during that match, and who knows that Mr Burnett might not have prejudged events at Twickenham subsequently. As a result of the sending off, play became brutal, and others could have been dismissed for violent acts of play. Wales totally dominated proceedings with two fine tries – Alan Phillips charged down a Steve Smith kick, fed Elgan Rees, who raced over for the score; whilst the captain himself claimed the other. England just couldn't score a try – they were completely outplayed but thanks to three Dusty Hare penalty goals claimed the win. They went on to win their first Grand Slam since 1957.

(Editor: I unfortunately failed to track down Jeff Squire)

Mark Taylor

Profile

Mark was the complete package. His balanced running was done at pace and given the smallest amount of space he could leave opponents in his wake. But he also possessed unfailing judgement. Gibbs and Taylor were an awesome centre partnership for Swansea and Wales, never more so than in the All Whites's comprehensive defeat of Llanelli in the 1999 SWALEC Cup Final at Ninian Park. I for one, however, will never forget his performance at St Helen's in a Heineken Cup encounter against the high-flying Wasps in 2000. Without his approach work and distribution, Matthew Robinson would never have crossed for his first half hat-trick of tries.

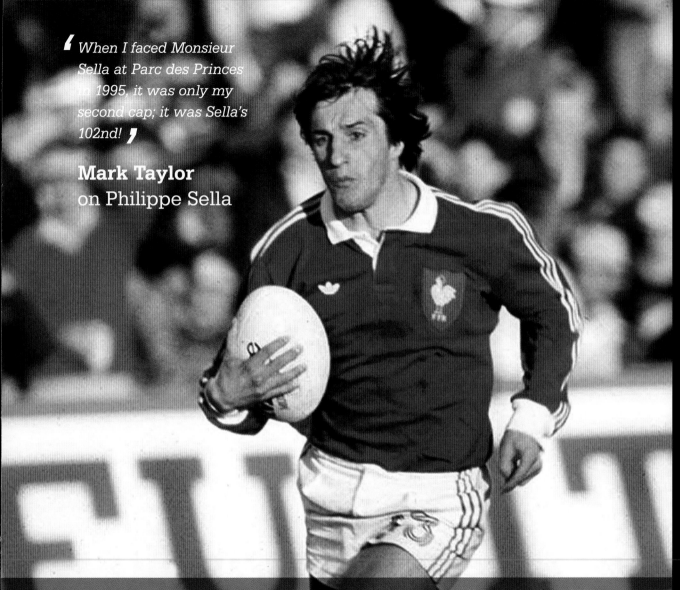

When I faced Monsieur Sella at Parc des Princes in 1995, it was only my second cap; it was Sella's 102nd!

Mark Taylor
on Philippe Sella

Q Which was your first match as captain?
A **Wales 50 Samoa 6, November 11, 2000 (Cardiff). It was Wales's first win against Samoa since 1988 and we succeeded in shrugging off the hoodoo of two Rugby World Cup defeats against the South Sea islanders. I was particularly nervous prior to the game as I'd had very little experience of captaincy.**

Q Which was your finest hour as a rugby player?
A **(i) Wales 12 South Africa 20, November 26, 1994 (Cardiff). My first cap. I was a Pontypool player at that time.
(ii) Wales 29 South Africa 19, June 26, 1999 (Cardiff). A game of historical significance – the first international played at the Millennium Stadium and Wales's first victory over South Africa. And I was the first to score a try at the ground!**

**(iii) Wales 32 Ireland 20, March 19, 2005 (Cardiff). I was as surpised as everyone when I featured in the crucial Six Nations Grand Slam decider against Ireland in 2005. I hadn't played for six months as a result of a bout of chicken pox which resulted in laser surgery on my eyes. It was quite funny really when Kevin Maggs tackled me early on and remarked, 'What are you doing here?'
(iv) Winning the Guinness Premiership title with Sale in 2006; my only victory at Twickenham.**

Q Who were your most respected opponents?
A **Philippe Sella and Brian O'Driscoll.**

Q Who was the best captain you played under?
A **Scott Gibbs. He led from the front.**

Delme Thomas

Profile

Whenever a list is drawn up of the ten most famous players to have played for Llanelli RFC, the name Delme Thomas invariably appears in the top five. Physically he was a giant of a man, excelling at the line-out where his upper body strength was such that he was able to outmanoeuvre the opposition. That robust physique also meant that he was no mean scrummager and was often an immense presence at rucks and mauls. For all his superhuman powers on the field, however, the man mountain from Bancyfelin was the gentlest, most reliable and highly respected person off it.

Q Which was your first match as captain?

A **Wales 16 New Zealand 19, December 2, 1972 (Cardiff). We contrived to lose a match where we started as firm favourites. We should have won convincingly. Yes, I know the players and supporters felt that referee Johnny Johnson should have awarded a try to fullback J.P.R. Williams rather than penalise him. However, we were our own worst enemies and should have turned pressure into points.**

Q Which was your finest hour as a rugby player?

A **(i) One Sunday afternoon in April 1966, I arrivied at my home village of Bancyfelin. It was usually quiet on Sundays especially between Sunday School and the Evening Service. Not that Sunday, however. Hundreds of people were milling around and I was engulfed and congratulated by an enthusiastic crowd of family, friends, neighbours, photographers, reporters and the like who** informed me of my selection for the British Lions to tour New Zealand!

(ii) Llanelli 9 New Zealand 3, October 31, 1972 (Stradey Park). In the dressing room the squad was ready for the fray. My words were simple and straightforward: 'We're wearing the Scarlet shirt. We're representing our community, our town, our county and our country. We have an opportunity to create history.'

(iii) Being part of the British Lions' series win in New Zealand in 1971.

(iv) 1971 Grand Slam success achieved under coach Clive Rowlands.

Q Who was your schoolboy rugby hero?

A **C.L. 'Cowboy' Davies from my home village of Bancyfelin.**

Q Who were your most respected opponents?

A **I respected them all but I have to mention brothers Colin and Stan Meads, Brian Price, Ian Ford and Keith Rowlands.**

Gareth Thomas

Profile

Mightily effective. The words to describe the Bridgend, Celtic Warriors, Cardiff, Stade Toulousain, Blues, Wales, British and Irish Lions, and now Celtic Crusaders fullback, centre and wing three-quarter. Physically a man mountain, 'Alfie', as he is known, was also elusive, powerful and unpredictable, with a turn of speed which left defenders trailing in his wake. A Heineken Cup winner in 2006, his playing career has been successful, profitable and sometimes clouded in controversy – I venture to add that there might just be an *Alfie 2* film at a cinema near you in the not too distant future!

Beating England at Cardiff has always meant everything for Welshmen. This was especially true of Gareth Thomas in 2005, as Wales took their first step towards their first Grand Slam for 27 years.

FINEST HOURS AS A RUGBY PLAYER

(i) First cap and three tries against Japan at Bloemfontein during Rugby World Cup 1995.

(ii) Captaining Wales during the 2005 Grand Slam season – it must have been particularly disappointing for Gareth to have broken his arm during the match against France at the Stade de France.

(iii) Leading the British and Irish Lions in the last two Test Matches (and for 78 minutes of the First Test) out in New Zealand in 2005.

(iv) Gareth is the only Welshman – and one of only 14 players ever – to have won over a hundred international caps. The former Australian scrum half and captain George Gregan leads the way with 139.

(v) A Heineken Cup winners medal for Stade Toulousain. Gareth played on the left wing for the French club in the tenth Heineken Final at Murrayfield in May 2005 when Toulouse beat Stade Français by 18 points to 12.

(vi) Four tries in a 60-21 victory for Wales against Italy at Treviso in 1999.

(vii) An EDF final win for the Cardiff Blues at Twickenham in 2009 – Blues 50 Gloucester 12.

(viii) First Super League try in a 20-14 win for the Celtic Crusaders against Wakefield in April 2010.

George Gregan (middle), Gareth Thomas's fellow cap centurion, celebrates with his Australian teammates against Scotland.

Malcolm Thomas

Profile

They came from near and far to Rodney Parade. Newport in the early 1950s were a delight to watch with a philosophy based on all-out attack. Outside half Roy Burnett possessed that spark of genius whilst Olympian Ken Jones was widely acknowledged as one of the finest and fastest wing three-quarters in world rugby. They also had a catalyst in Malcolm Thomas whose control, pace and balanced running often left opponents in his wake. The Machen born centre-threequarter, who was named after the record-breaking racing driver, Malcolm Campbell, was also a shrewd tactical kicker and accurate place kicker who broke records as an individual points scorer with the 1950 and 1959 British Lions in New Zealand.

Ken Jones, Malcolm Thomas's fellow Newport three-quarter, Welsh international and British Lion.

Paul Thorburn

Profile

Paul Thorburn was a fine fullback and a prolific goal-kicker, who kicked the longest ever penalty goal in rugby history for Wales against Scotland in the Five Nations Championship at the National Stadium in Cardiff in 1986. The kick measured exactly 70 yards eight-and-a-half-inches (64.2m). His magnificent conversion of Adrian Hadley's last-minute try secured a 21-20 victory against Australia and provided Wales with a creditable third place in the 1987 Rugby World Cup Finals. He was tournament director for the 1999 World Cup when Wales hosted the event, and has also worked as special projects manager for the Welsh Rugby Union.

(From l. to r.) The late Brian Williams, Adrian Varney and John Davies hold Kevin Phillips aloft, as Paul Thorburn's Neath celebrate another Heineken League victory.

Q Which was your best match as captain?

A **Wales 12 England 9, March 18, 1989 (Cardiff). A victory would have given the old enemy the championship but thanks to Robert Norster's line-out skills and Robert Jones's box kicks we managed to scrape a victory. Mike Hall claimed the game's solitary try – a disputed touchdown when Rory Underwood's pass to Jon Webb went astray.**

Q Which was your finest hour as a rugby player?

A **Wales 22 Australia 21, June 18, 1987 (Rotorua). In the Rugby World Cup Third Place Play Off at Rotorua. Australia were leading 21-16 with seconds remaining when Adrian Hadley dived in at the corner after a bout of passing which could only be described as typically Welsh.**

Q Who was the first name on your team sheet?

A **Mine, of course!**

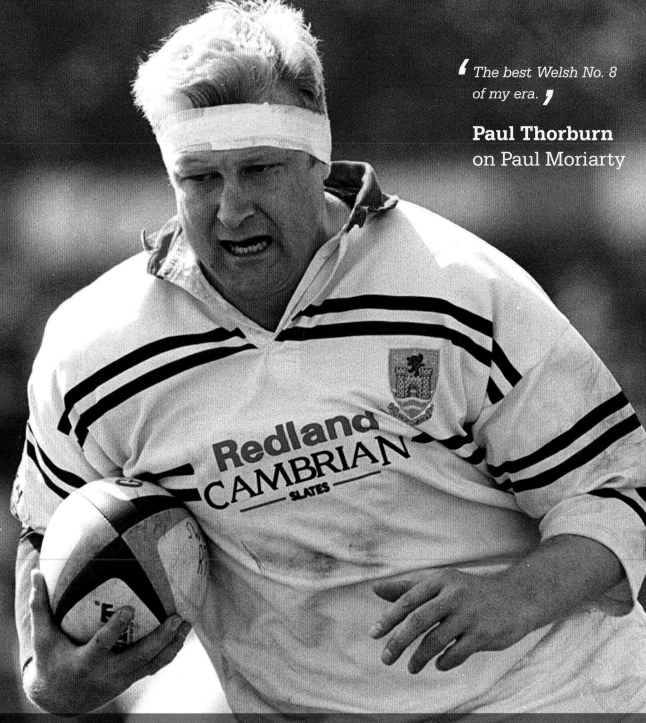

‛ The best Welsh No. 8 of my era. ’

Paul Thorburn
on Paul Moriarty

Q Which current Welsh player would you love to have in your team?

A **Shane Williams. Despite there being limited space on the field these days, he has the ability to create something from nothing.**

Q Which current non-Welsh player would you love to have in your team?

A **Tommy Bowe. Not only does he provide a cutting edge and has scored and created great tries, he is a very genuine guy whom I enjoy being around.**

Q Who was the best captain you played under?

A **Richard Moriarty**

David Watkins

Profile

David Watkins graced the fields of Monmouthshire, Wales, Great Britain and the rugby world during the 1960s and 1970s where his ball skills were evident for all to see. He was a star in the making – someone who with his style of play could hypnotise opposition and onlookers alike. He was lightning fast off the mark and was blessed with a sidestep that could deceive any opponent. He won his first cap for Wales in 1963, played six times for the British Lions, was captain when Keith Jarrett, an 18-year-old schoolboy, scored 19 points on his Welsh debut against England in April 1967, and crowned an illustrious career when he captained the Great Britain rugby league side on their tour of Australia in 1975.

Hugely confident, commanding respect from all around him. Not so much an Austin Healey, more of an Aston Martin!

David Watkins
on Austin Healey

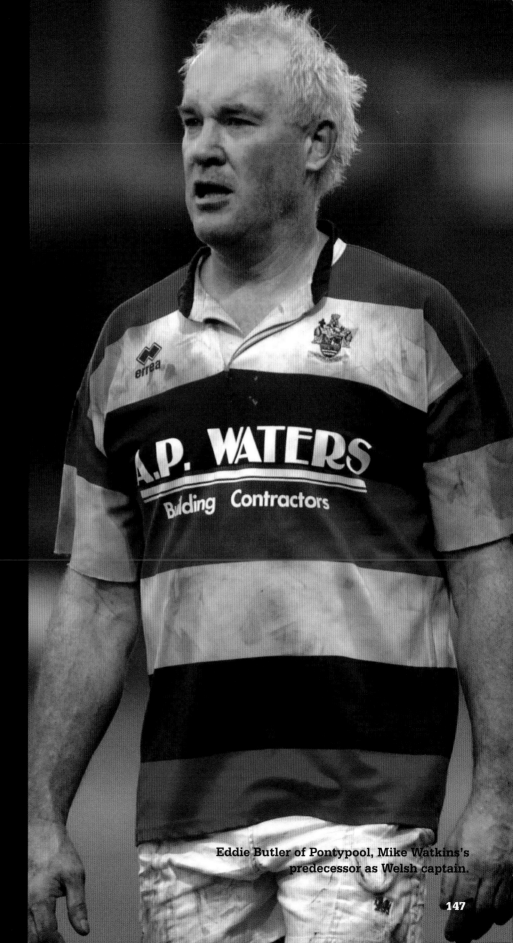

Mike Watkins

Profile

How many players have made their debut for Wales as captain? Only five, and they include Mike Watkins, the former Newport and Wales hooker. A natural leader who captained his club side from 1983-87, he first appeared on the international scene in 1976 when he played for Wales B. A tour to Australia followed in 1978 when 'Spikey' played in four regional matches but never wore the red jersey in a test match – the main reason being one Bobby Windsor, who was a permanent fixture in the front row. As Mike commented dryly, 'I could never get on because Bobby would never come off!' It would take another six years for the call to come: 'Mike you're in the team as CAPTAIN!'

Eddie Butler of Pontypool, Mike Watkins's predecessor as Welsh captain.

J.P.R. Williams

Profile

George Nepia, Bob Scott, Terry Davies, Don Clarke, Ken Scotland, Jim Lenehan, Terry Price, Bob Hiller, Pierre Villepreux, Andy Irvine, Serge Blanco, Gavin Hastings, Christian Cullen, Matt Burke, Percy Montgomery, Mils Muliaina, Rob Kearney, Clément Poitreneaud and Lee Byrne. All great fullbacks. But none as great as J.P.R. Williams of London Welsh, Bridgend, Wales and the British Lions. He was fearless under the high ball, totally committed in all defensive situations and a true master of the counter-attack. In the early days, fullbacks wore No.1 on their backs. But even when JPR wore No. 15, he was still Number One.

JPR with his fellow medic and
British Lion, Jamie Roberts.

Q Which was your best match as captain?
A **Scotland 13 Wales 19, January 20, 1979 (Murrayfield). The Welsh forwards played superbly with the Pontypool front row to the fore. Andy Irvine crossed for a first-half try but we sealed the win with tries from Elgan Rees and Terry Holmes.**

Q Which was your finest hour as a rugby player?
A **Winning Lions tours in New Zealand in 1971 and South Africa in 1974 [Editor: JPR's sensational drop goal in the Final Test in Auckland in 1971 secured a 14-14 draw for the British Lions and a series win – still the only occasion the Lions have returned victorious**

Q Who would have been the first name on your team sheet?
A **Gareth Edwards**

Q Which current Welsh player would you love to have in your team?
A **Shane Williams. A brilliant try-scorer.**

Q Which current non-Welsh player would you love to have in your team?
A **Brian O'Driscoll**

Q Who was the best captain you faced?
A **Wille John McBride**

Q Who was the best captain you played under?

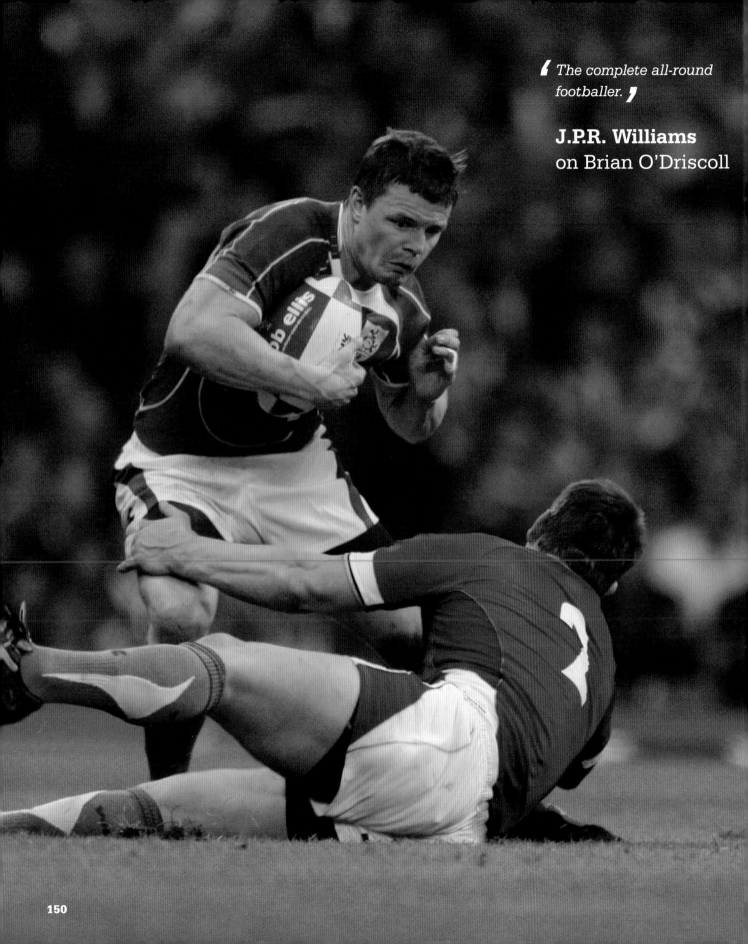

Lloyd Williams

Profile

Lloyd Williams was the Mike Phillips of the 1950s and early 1960s. He could have played with some distinction as a flank forward such was his power, physique, and boundless energy. Like Haydn Tanner and Rex Willis before him, Lloyd Williams captained his club and country, playing 13 times for Wales and an impressive 310 games for Cardiff. He was unlucky not to be chosen to tour New Zealand in 1959, beacuse when conditions were at their worst, Lloyd was at his best! He was one of eight brothers to play for Cardiff, another of whom, Bleddyn, was hailed 'The Prince of Centres'.

Lloyd Williams' brother Bleddyn, 'The Prince of Centres'.

Martyn Williams

Profile

Here in Wales and beyond, Martyn Williams is described by the knowledgeable and well-informed as one of the best open side wing-forwards to have played the game. Determined and brave, a skilled scavenger and flawless footballer, the red-headed forward has a natural talent that has left the rugby purists purring. There have been many high points in his outstanding career, none more so than the clinching try in the 2008 Grand Slam season where he displayed Colin Jackson's hurdling skills to get to the try line. His nickname 'Nugget' says it all.

Ospreys teammates Tommy Bowe and Shane Williams match each other stride for stride for their respective international teams, Ireland and Wales.

Q Which was your first match as captain?
A **Scotland 13 Wales 26, February 8, 2009 (Edinburgh) It was an honour to captain the side in the absence of Ryan Jones who withdrew only hours before kick-off. It proved a confusing task introducing the team to Princess Anne prior to the anthems, as we had four Joneses, two Williamses and one Rees in the starting line-up: 'Jones, another Jones Ma'am, Williams, yet another Jones…' And so it went on!**

Q Which was your finest hour as a rugby player?
A **The Grand Slam victory against Ireland in 2005 was special. The rugby we played throughout the tournament was simply outstanding, especially the victory at Stade de France. However, the realisation at the final whistle at the Millennium Stadium that we had achieved our goal was the icing on the** cake. It was, and still is, a significant episode in my rugby career. And we managed to repeat the feat in 2008!

Q Who would be the first name on your team sheet?
A **Shane Williams. A unique matchwinner.**

Q Which current non-Welsh player would you love to have in your team?
A **Brian O'Driscoll. Simply the best centre three-quarter of his generation.**

Q Who is the best captain you've faced?
A **Martin Johnson**

Q Who is your most respected opponent?
A **Richie McCaw**

Q Who is the best captain you've played under?
A **Paul O'Connell**

Martyn Williams's British Lions captain Paul O'Connell
attempts to escape the clutches of Jamie Roberts

David Young

Profile

Not for the faint-hearted, what goes on in the front row of a scrum is a secret known only to a select few. It is an apprenticeship with specialised knowledge passed on through word of mouth and the education of actions. David (Dai) Young was accepted by opponents worldwide as a master of the craft of the tight-head prop forward, a position in which quality players are as rare as red squirrels. David's compulsion to strain nerve and sinew saw him win over fifty caps for Wales as well as representing the British and Irish Lions on three tours in 1989, 1997 and 2001.

> *An iconic figure I respected enormously.*
>
> David Young
> on Graham Price

Q Which was your first match as captain?

A **Wales 3 France 36, February 5, 2000 (Cardiff) I had to scour the record books to remind me! It was the international debut of Shane Williams, who replaced Dafydd James in the final quarter. I became the first prop forward to captain Wales since John Lloyd back in 1972.**

Q Which was your finest hour as a rugby player?

A **(i) Wales 16 England 3, June 8, 1987 (Ballymore) That first cap was rather special – it was a Rugby World Cup quarter final! I was not in the original party but when Stuart Evans broke his foot against Tonga, I was conveniently available as I'd travelled to Australia to play for Northern Suburbs. I was just nineteen years of age at the time. (ii) The ovation I received from the Salford fans prior to the St Helens match when it was announced I'd been chosen to captain the Welsh Rugby League team against France in 1995.**

(iii) I don't normally do nostalgia but coming off the bench at Wembley in 1999 and being part of a great win against England would have to be a great rugby moment, as was Wales's first win against South Africa in 1999, mind. (iv) Salford's magnificent win against Wigan in the Challenge Cup Quarter Final at the Willows. (v) My fiftieth cap, against Argentina in Cardiff, when my three boys accompanied me on to the field as mascots.

Q Who was your most respected opponent?

A **Steve McDowell (New Zealand)**

Q Who were the best captains you played under?

A **Mark Davies (my first captain at Swansea), Bob Norster, who was so helpful and commanded respect, Rob Howley, who read the game so well, and my captain and coach at Salford, Gary Jack.**

> *His spirit, strength of character, determination and all-round genius on the field made him a cult hero.*

David Young
on Jonathan Davies

Acknowledgements

Thanks to all who responded so helpfully to requests for information, sources and material, and those who made difficult tasks so much simpler for all concerned, among them Bethan John-Sinclair, Gareth Rees, Owain Talfryn Jones, Jill Bevan, Sue Evans, Ben Evans, Gareth Everett, Matthew Phillips, Paul Rose, Huw John Hughes, John Harris, David Jones, J.J. Williams, Steve Lewis, Mainstream Publishing, Media Wales, *Glamorgan Gazette*, *South Wales Argus*, *South Wales Evening Post*, Press Association, and James Pinniger and Andrew Cowie at Colorsport.

Thanks especially to the photographers, agencies and individuals for their permission to reproduce the photographs in this book – most refusing to accept payment for their services. In those instances where it was impossible to trace the owners, the Editors and the Publishers urge the relevant individuals to contact Gomer to make sure that their contributions be recognized in any subsequent reprints of *Welsh Rugby Captains*.

Huw Evans Agency: ii, 13, 14-15, 16, 17, 19, 20 (r.), 21, 22, 23, 24-5, 26, 28 (l.), 29, 30 (r.), 31, 33, 34 (r.), 35, 38, 39, 40 (l.), 42-43, 44 (l.) 45, 46 (l.), 50 (l.), 51, 54, 58 (r.), 59, 62-63, 64, 65, 66, 68, 70-71, 72, 73, 74-75, 77, 78, 79 (r.), 80, 81, 82, 83, 84, 85, 86, 87, 92, 93, 94-95, 96, 97, 98, 99, 100 (r.), 101, 102 (r.), 103, 105, 106 (r.), 107, 110-111, 112, 114, 115, 116, 117, 118, 119 (r.), 120 (l.), 121, 125, 126, 127, 130-131, 134, 136,137, 138, 139, 140-141, 143 ,145, 146, 148, 149, 150, 151,152, 153, 154-155, 156, 158-159.
Colorsport: iii, iv, 12, 27, 32, 36-37, 40 (r.), 41, 44 (r.), 48-49, 50 (r.), 52-53, 55, 56-57, 67, 69, 89, 90-91, 100 (l.); 108 (Barry John), 113 (r.), 122, 123, 131-132, 135.
Alun Wyn Bevan: 10-1118 (r.), 45 (l.), 60 (r.), 76 (l.), 79 (l.), 102 (l.), 113 (l.).
Jimmy Giddings: 12 (l.).
Western Mail/Media Wales: 16, 28 (r.), 30, 34, 88 (r.), 119 (l.), 132 (l.),
David Jones/ Press Association: 76 (r.).
John Harris: 88 (l.), 120 (r.),
Robert Evans: 108 (Lewis Jones),
South Wales Argus: 108 (Ken Jones), 142 (r.), 147.
Bryn Campbell: 124.
South Wales Evening Post: 144

And last but not least, thanks to the 61 Welsh rugby captains still alive whose enthusiasm and willingness to contribute made this book possible.